Cayman Islands

WORLD BIBLIOGRAPHICAL SERIES

General Editors:

Robert G. Neville (Executive Editor)

John J. Horton

Robert A. Myers   Hans H. Wellisch

Ian Wallace   Ralph Lee Woodward, Jr.

John J. Horton is Deputy Librarian of the University of Bradford and was formerly Chairman of its Academic Board of Studies in Social Sciences. He has maintained a longstanding interest in the discipline of area studies and its associated bibliographical problems, with special reference to European Studies. In particular he has published in the field of Icelandic and of Yugoslav studies, including the two relevant volumes in the World Bibliographical Series.

Robert A. Myers is Associate Professor of Anthropology in the Division of Social Sciences and Director of Study Abroad Programs at Alfred University, Alfred, New York. He has studied post-colonial island nations of the Caribbean and has spent two years in Nigeria on a Fulbright Lectureship. His interests include international public health, historical anthropology and developing societies. In addition to *Amerindians of the Lesser Antilles: a bibliography* (1981), *A Resource Guide to Dominica, 1493-1986* (1987) and numerous articles, he has compiled the World Bibliographical Series volumes on *Dominica* (1987), *Nigeria* (1989) and *Ghana* (1991).

Ian Wallace is Professor of German at the University of Bath. A graduate of Oxford in French and German, he also studied in Tübingen, Heidelberg and Lausanne before taking teaching posts at universities in the USA, Scotland and England. He specializes in contemporary German affairs, especially literature and culture, on which he has published numerous articles and books. In 1979 he founded the journal *GDR Monitor*, which he continues to edit under its new title *German Monitor*.

Hans H. Wellisch is Professor emeritus at the College of Library and Information Services, University of Maryland. He was President of the American Society of Indexers and was a member of the International Federation for Documentation. He is the author of numerous articles and several books on indexing and abstracting, and has published *The Conversion of Scripts and Indexing and Abstracting: an International Bibliography*, and *Indexing from A to Z*. He also contributes frequently to *Journal of the American Society for Information Science*, *The Indexer* and other professional journals.

Ralph Lee Woodward, Jr. is Professor of History at Tulane University, New Orleans. He is the author of *Central America, a Nation Divided*, 2nd ed. (1985), as well as several monographs and more than seventy scholarly articles on modern Latin America. He has also compiled volumes in the World Bibliographical Series on *Belize* (1980), *El Salvador* (1988), *Guatemala* (Rev. Ed.) (1992) and *Nicaragua* (Rev. Ed.) (1994). Dr. Woodward edited the Central American section of the *Research Guide to Central America and the Caribbean* (1985) and is currently associate editor of Scribner's *Encyclopedia of Latin American History*.

VOLUME 187

Cayman Islands

Paul G. Boultbee

Compiler

CLIO PRESS

OXFORD, ENGLAND · SANTA BARBARA, CALIFORNIA
DENVER, COLORADO

British Library Cataloguing in Publication Data

Boultbee, Paul G.
Cayman Islands – (World bibliographical series; v. 187)
1. Cayman Islands – Bibliography
I. Title
016.9′7′2921

ISBN 1–85109–240–4

ABC-CLIO Ltd.,
Old Clarendon Ironworks,
35A Great Clarendon Street,
Oxford OX2 6AT, England.

ABC-CLIO Inc.,
130 Cremona Drive,
Santa Barbara,
CA 93116, USA

Designed by Bernard Crossland.
Typeset by Columns Design and Production Services Ltd., Reading, England.
Printed and bound in Great Britain by Bookcraft (Bath) Ltd., Midsomer Norton.

THE WORLD BIBLIOGRAPHICAL SERIES

This series, which is principally designed for the English speaker, will eventually cover every country (and many of the world's principal regions), each in a separate volume comprising annotated entries on works dealing with its history, geography, economy and politics; and with its people, their culture, customs, religion and social organization. Attention will also be paid to current living conditions – housing, education, newspapers, clothing, etc.– that are all too often ignored in standard bibliographies; and to those particular aspects relevant to individual countries. Each volume seeks to achieve, by use of careful selectivity and critical assessment of the literature, an expression of the country and an appreciation of its nature and national aspirations, to guide the reader towards an understanding of its importance. The keynote of the series is to provide, in a uniform format, an interpretation of each country that will express its culture, its place in the world, and the qualities and background that make it unique. The views expressed in individual volumes, however, are not necessarily those of the publisher.

VOLUMES IN THE SERIES

For Grandma and Aunt Connie
With gratitude and love

Contents

Contents

Contents

Introduction

The Cayman Islands, a Crown Colony of the United Kingdom, lie about 290 kilometres west-north-west of Jamaica and consist of three main islands: Grand Cayman, on which is situated the capital of George Town; Little Cayman; and Cayman Brac. Although all three islands are inhabited, the majority of the population lives on Grand Cayman. According to the 1989 census, the total population was 25,355. Of this number, 23,881 people lived on Grand Cayman (12,921 in the capital of George Town), 1441 on Cayman Brac, and 33 on Little Cayman.

All three islands are an outcropping of the Cayman Ridge, a submarine mountain range that extends west from the Sierra Maestra mountain range in Cuba. They are low-lying and composed of limestone and coral. The vegetation is primarily scrub with some mangrove swamp areas. The islands themselves are not very large. Grand Cayman is 197 square kilometres, while Cayman Brac and Little Cayman cover 36 square kilometres and 26 square kilometres, respectively. Little Cayman and Cayman Brac lie 89 miles north-east of Grand Cayman. These two sister islands, as they are known, are separated from each other by a seven-mile wide channel. The climate is tropical with a rainy season extending from May to October. Hurricanes pose a threat from midsummer to November.

Christopher Columbus first sighted Little Cayman and Cayman Brac on 10 May 1503 on his fourth and last voyage. He named them 'Las Tortugas' because of all the turtles which were found there. A 1523 map labels them 'Lagartos' meaning alligator or large lizard, an allusion to the iguanas still found on Cayman Brac. By 1530 they were known as Caymanas (or Caymanus) after the Carib word for the marine crocodiles which lived there. The first recorded English visitor was Sir Francis Drake who, in 1586, searched the islands looking for fresh meat for his crew. However, he did not claim the islands for

England and the Caymans remained under Spanish control until they were ceded, along with Jamaica, to the English under the terms of the Treaty of Madrid in 1670.

There are no records to indicate that the islands at the time of their discovery, were or had been inhabited by any of the aboriginals found on other Caribbean islands. Moreover, the Spanish made no attempt to settle the islands. In fact, the Caymans were originally seen only as a source for turtle meat. In the seventeenth and early eighteenth centuries, the islands were used by privateers as a base for their operations, even after privateering was outlawed in 1713. The English did not begin to settle on the islands until 1734 when the first royal grant of land was issued for Grand Cayman. These early settlers were primarily from Jamaica and earned their living from the sea as turtle fishermen, wreckers or ships' crews. As the Caymans began to be settled, they became a dependency of Jamaica. Permanent settlements on Little Cayman and Cayman Brac were not established until 1833.

In 1832 representative government was established and the Legislative Assembly first met. This assembly was located in Grand Cayman. There was no actual administrative link between Grand Cayman and the two other smaller islands until 1877 when a Justice of the Peace arrived on Cayman Brac.

The Cayman Islands remained a dependency of Jamaica until 4 July 1959 when they became a separate Crown Colony. However, the Governor of Jamaica still held responsibility for the islands until Jamaican independence in 1962. At this point, a separate administrator was appointed for the Cayman Islands (the title was changed to governor in 1971) and the area became dependent directly on the United Kingdom. The 1959 Constitution was revised in 1972, 1992, and 1994.

Given the islands' location, the tourist industry is the principal economic activity. Tourism began to increase in the 1960s and became an economic force by the 1980s. Now, more than half-a-million people visit the Cayman Islands annually and the industry accounts for upwards of 50% of the employment in the country.

Stable government and favourable banking laws have both played a large role in establishing the Cayman Islands as the world's largest offshore financial centre. Nearly 30,000 companies and more than 500 banks and trust companies are registered in the Caymans, along with approximately 350 insurance companies. The banking and finance sector employs one tenth of the labour force.

According to legend, the islands' tax free status dates from the

Wreck of the Ten Sails (1794) when islanders rushed to save passengers travelling to England from Jamaica. One of the passengers rescued was said to have been an unnamed royal personage. In gratitude, King George III decreed that Caymanians were henceforth free from conscription in wartime and free from personal taxation. Historical documentation does not support this widely-held belief.

There is some agriculture but it is limited due to infertile soil, low rainfall and high labour costs. Crops consist of citrus fruits and bananas as well as some other produce for local consumption. There is limited livestock rearing. The once vibrant turtle fishing industry has almost disappeared due to centuries of over-harvesting. One commercial turtle farm produces mainly for domestic consumption and acts as a research centre.

The Cayman Islands have existed in relative isolation from the rest of the world for centuries. The islands' history and the lives of its inhabitants have traditionally revolved around the sea. It has only been in the second half of the twentieth century that the Cayman Islands have become better known and understood. Tourism and offshore banking have opened the Caymans to the rest of the world. These two service industries will comprise the base upon which the islands will grow and prosper.

The Bibliography

The 447 entries have been grouped into thirty categories, with sub-categories, which are similar to those found in other volumes of the World Bibliographical Series.

All sections are arranged chronologically with the most recent items listed first. Two or more items published in the same year have been listed alphabetically by the first major word in the title. In some instances, particularly in the 'Literature' and 'History' sections, items published in the Cayman Islands have no discernible publication dates. These items have been listed at the end of the sections in alphabetical order by the first major word in the title.

The bibliography includes books, journal articles, and government documents. It does not include dissertations. Some of the items listed in this bibliography have been published in the Cayman Islands and are not always readily available outside the country. They are, however, available at the Cayman Islands National Archive (Crewe Road, Grand Cayman, Cayman Islands, British West Indies), the George Town Public Library (P. O. Box 1172G, George Town, Grand Cayman, Cayman Islands, British West Indies), or the International

Introduction

College of the Cayman Islands (Newlands, Grand Cayman, Cayman Islands, British West Indies).

Some subject sections are far larger than others. For instance, there are eighty-five entries under Geology (and its sub-categories) and 122 entries under Flora and Fauna. In contrast, the humanities and social sciences categories are far smaller. This is a reflection of the great interest shown by the scientific community.

Acknowledgements

I would like to express my thanks to all those who have helped me in the compilation of this bibliography. I was able to see a great deal of the material on a research trip to Grand Cayman. I would like to thank Dr. David Hughey, Dean of the International College of the Cayman Islands who opened the College's Library collection to me and gave me free rein to conduct my research. My thanks also to Michelle Fitzgerald of the Cayman Islands National Archive who enthusiastically welcomed me to that fine facility and made my work there so pleasant. Tamara Selzer of the Cayman Islands National Archive was also most helpful in making sure that I saw everything I needed.

I reserve a separate and heart-felt thanks to Rosalie Bachor of the Red Deer College Library who processed so many of my interlibrary loan requests and took it as a personal affront if all did not run smoothly.

Thanks are due once again to my wife, Glynis, who has always supported and encouraged my bibliographic research. Her suggestions and advice are always thoughtful and valuable and most appreciated.

Paul G. Boultbee
August 1995

The Country and Its People

1 **The postcards of the Cayman Islands, including Cayman Brac and drawings of Little Cayman.**
Ed Oliver.   Grand Cayman: EDO, 1993. 2 maps.
Reproduces 153 postcards depicting all aspects of life and scenery in the Cayman Islands.

2 **The Cambridge encyclopedia of Latin America and the Caribbean.**
Edited by Simon Collier, Thomas E. Skidmore, Harold Blakemore.
Cambridge: Cambridge University Press, 1992. 2nd ed. 479p. 60 maps.
bibliog.
This one volume encyclopedia treats its subject in six major thematic sections: the physical environment; the economy; the peoples; history; politics and society; and culture. Although the work primarily concentrates on Latin America and South America and contains only a little information specifically on the Cayman Islands, nonetheless it does offer good background information to the region.

3 **The Americas review.**
Saffron Walden, England: World of Information; Edison, New Jersey: Hunter Publishing, 1990-. annual.
This publication covers North America, Latin America, and the Caribbean and includes a section on each country which provides general information, a country profile, a business guide, and a map. It is a useful source of current and readily accessible factual details on the Cayman Islands. This periodical began publication in 1979 under the title, *Latin America Annual Review and the Caribbean*. It became *Latin America and Caribbean* in 1980 and was then re-titled *Latin America and Caribbean Review* in 1985 before the change to *The Americas Review* in 1990.

1

4   **The Cayman Islands: a social studies text.**
London: Macmillan Caribbean, 1989. 202p. 14 maps.
This is the first social studies textbook produced specifically for the children of the
Cayman Islands. It was written by a group of teachers and education officers in a
workshop setting. Using stories, letters, and diaries, the textbook explores geography,
climate, flora and fauna, history, government, culture and heritage, tourism, banking
and insurance, and transport and communication.

5   **Islands of the Commonwealth Caribbean: a regional study.**
Edited by Sandra Meditz, Dennis M. Hanratty.   Washington, DC:
Federal Research Division, Library of Congress, 1989. 771p. 19 maps.
bibliog. (Area Handbook Series) (DA Pam., 550-33).
Information on the Cayman Islands is found in the chapter, 'British dependencies: The
Cayman Islands and the Turks and Caicos Islands' (p. 561-83). The chapter treats
these two dependencies together and is divided into sections on geography,
population, education, health and welfare, the economy, government and politics,
foreign relations, and national security.

6   **Which way to the islands?**
H. George Nowak.   Canton, Ohio: Daring Books, 1988. 239p. map.
Nowak, also known as 'The Barefoot Man', a Cayman Island entertainer and author,
provides a collection of humorous anecdotes. These portray a simplified logic and
wisdom applicable not only to Cayman Islanders but indeed to islanders throughout
the world.

7   **The people time forgot: a photographic portrayal of the people of the
Cayman Islands.**
H. George Nowak, Roy Bodden, Henry George.   Grand Cayman:
Cayman Free Press, 1987. 1 vol.
The evocative and sensitive black-and white-photographs in this book are a wonderful
tribute to the people of the Cayman Islands. Each photograph is accompanied by a
short caption.

8   **Beautiful isles Cayman.**
Paul Humann.   Grand Cayman: Hobbies & Books, 1986. 104p. 2 maps.
Humann presents a selection of colour photographs divided into the following topics:
history, scenic Cayman, underwater, people, government, commerce and industry, and
tourism. Each section includes a short introductory text.

9   **Fair skies for the Cayman Islands.**
Peter Benchley.   *National Geographic*, vol. 167, no. 6 (June 1985),
p. 798-824.
Benchley describes the Cayman Islands as a tourist resort, a diving mecca, a banking
centre and a tax haven, and his text is accompanied by fascinating colour photographs.

10 **South America, Central America, and the Caribbean.**
London: Europa, 1985-. biennial.
This is an excellent quick-reference source for all countries in South and Central America and the Caribbean. Background articles contain material on both the region and its organizations. Entries for each country include statistics as well as information on history, politics and government, religion, the media, finance and banking, trade and industry, tourism and education.

11 **A visit to Grand Cayman.**
Paul Humann.   Grand Cayman: Hobbies & Books, [n.d.] 48p. 2 maps.
The author's text is accompanied by colour photographs depicting diving, the island scenery, flora, the people, and government buildings.

12 **The Cayman Islands: in full colour.**
Hans W. Hannau.   London: Robert Hale, 1978. 64p. 3 maps.
Hannau's books are most notable for their full-colour plates and this is no exception. However, this is a small handbook and therefore the fifty-four plates, while quite lovely, are not very large. The text provides information about history and geography, government and politics, finance and commerce, as well as tourism and sporting activities.

13 **'Nell Connor, here': a woman at work in the Cayman Islands.**
Ronald Fouts, Morris Jackson.   Washington, DC: Ram Publications, 1978. 1 vol.
The Nell Connor referred to in the title is a basket weaver. The thirty-one colour plates which make up this book portray Nell, her work, and island life in general. The work does not include a text.

14 **Caribbean year book.**
Toronto: Caribook, 1977/78-. annual.
This annual reference book was first published in 1926/27 under the title *Year book of the West Indies and countries of the Caribbean*. In 1953 the title was changed to *West Indies and Caribbean year book*. It is a very good quick-reference source for the Cayman Islands, as well as for other countries in the Caribbean region. It includes information on government, public and social services, public utilities, communications, natural resources, industries, finance, trade and commerce, newspapers and periodicals, and travel and tourism. There is also a business directory.

15 **Cayman the affluent climate.**
John Wright.   *Geographical Magazine*, vol. 49, no. 4 (Jan. 1977), p. 262-64.
Wright describes the islands' geography and geology and provides information on population, industry, land ownership and the environment.

16 **A view of the Cayman Islands.**
Alan H. Donald. *Corona*, vol. 13, no. 1 (Jan. 1961), p. 9-12.

When Donald wrote this article, the Cayman Islands were on the verge of opening up to the outside world. Air travel to the islands was just beginning and the tourist industry was in its infancy. He points out that the islanders had little use either for independence or the West Indian Federation and comments on the political administration of the islands and the moral and ethical issues that the country would soon have to face.

17 **Cayman Islands: report for the years . . . .**
Great Britain. Foreign and Commonwealth Office.   London: HMSO, 1958-. annual.

These annual reports provide a wealth of textual and statistical information about the following topics: population, finance and taxation, currency and banking, commerce and industry, social services, legislation, justice, communications, public utilities, the press, geography and climate, history, and government administration.

18 **Cayman Islands – a sketch.**
Edwin Beal Doran, Jr.   *Caribbean*, vol. 10, no. 2 (Sept. 1956), p. 31-32, 42.

Doran provides brief comments on climate, topography, vegetation, history, and commerce.

19 **Lazy days in the sun.**
Claud Morris.   *Canada-West Indies Magazine*, vol. 29, no. 8 (Aug. 1940), p. 25-27, 29.

Morris was a London journalist who was sent to the West Indies to recover from war wounds. This article presents his impressions of various Caymanian subjects.

20 **Turtles and postage stamps.**
Glanville Smith.   *The Atlantic Monthly*, vol. 160, no. 3 (Sept. 1937), p. 347-50.

The author discusses the value of turtles and postage stamps to the economy of the Cayman Islands. The observations are based on a short visit he made there in the early 1930s.

21 **Life and adventures in the West Indies.**
Vaquero, pseud.   London: John Bale, Sons & Danielsson, 1914.
284p. 8 maps.

Vaquero's book is 'a friendly effort to portray, by means of words and pictures, the beauty, the commercial products and the people of the West Indian Islands.' The author, who was believed to have been the Government Medical Officer to the Cayman Islands, gives a very good description of life in the early twentieth century and provides an excellent commentary on Caymanian society. The Cayman Islands are described in chapters 2 and 3. Also included in the volume are six very good black-and-white photographs. There is some evidence to suggest that Vaquero's real name was Richard Keatinge. He was employed as Medical Officer in 1906 and some events related in the book correspond to events which occurred during his tenure as Government Medical Officer. It is also known that Vaquero remained in Cayman for less than a year as did Dr Keatinge. Keatinge's predecessor, Dr F. R. Evans, also stayed for less than one year, so it is possible that he too could have been the physician behind the pseudonym.

Geography

22 Climate and tides of the Cayman Islands.
F. J. Burton. In: *The Cayman Islands: natural history and biogeography*. Edited by M. A. Brunt, J. E. Davies. Dordrecht, Netherlands: Kluwer Academic, 1994, p. 51-60. (Monographiae Biologicae, vol. 71).

Burton discusses temperature, evaporation and humidity, rainfall, wind, tides, and hurricanes. There are also several tables of information concerning: daily readings of maximum and minimum temperatures, wind speed and direction, evaporation, maximum and minimum water temperatures, solar radiation from 1973 to 1987; rainfall from 1914 to 1987; average tide elevations from 1976 to 1985; and severe hurricanes from 1662 to 1988.

23 The atlas of Central America and the Caribbean.
Diagram Group. New York: Macmillan; London: Collier Macmillan, 1985. 144p. 91 maps. bibliog.

This atlas is divided into three sections: an introduction and overview; the Central American nations; and the Caribbean nations. For each nation examined, the editors provide a text in which history, land use, population, health and education, social welfare, government and politics, and the economy are surveyed. Also included are a detailed physical map, a picture of the national flag and seal, and basic statistical data. Where appropriate, there are charts and tables for such elements as gross national product, imports and exports, land use, crops, and climate.

24 The maritime geography of the Cayman Islands.
Roger C. Smith. *Caribbean Geography*, vol. 1, no. 4 (1984), p. 247-55.

Smith describes the maritime geography of the Cayman Islands and the effect it has had on settlement patterns. The geography has predetermined the seaward perspective of the people throughout the islands' history. Because of their position in the Caribbean Sea, the islands were originally used as a provisioning way station. After settlement, the sea provided for turtling and wrecking, both of which became important to the people and their economy.

25 Hurricanes of the Caribbean and adjacent regions, 1492-1800.
Jose Carlos Millas.   Miami, Florida: Academy of the Arts and Sciences of the Americas, 1968. 328p. map. bibliog.

In this fascinating study, Millas examines contemporary documents pertaining to 308 recorded hurricanes which allegedly occurred in the Caribbean between 1492 and 1800. He concludes that forty-five of the cases reported lack sufficient evidence to be considered true hurricanes. While Fassig (q.v.) reviews hurricanes primarily in a general sense in his *Hurricanes of the West Indies*, Millas examines the individual hurricanes in some detail.

26 Hurricanes of the West Indies.
Oliver Lanard Fassig.   Washington, DC: Government Printing Office, 1913. 28p. 17 maps. (US Department of Agriculture. Weather Bureau. Bulletin X. W. B., 487).

In this report, Fassig concentrates on those storms which swept through the Caribbean between 1876 and 1911. He concludes that eighty-eight percent of the hurricanes appear in August, September and October and have an average duration of six days. He also provides information on their origins and movements. The maps trace all of the hurricanes under examination. Fassig also pays particular attention to the devastating hurricane of 7-20 August 1899.

27 West Indian hurricanes.
Edward Bennett Garriott.   Washington, DC: Weather Bureau, 1900. 69p. (US Department of Agriculture. Weather Bureau. Bulletin H. W. B., 232).

This report reviews the writings of the more prominent meteorologists of the nineteenth century insofar as they refer to tropical storms of the North Atlantic and presents a chronological list of West Indian storms from 1493 to 1900. There are also descriptions of some of the more important hurricanes.

28 A historical geography of the British colonies.
Charles Prestwood Lucas.   Oxford: Clarendon, 1887-1920. 7 vols.

Volume two (1905) contains information on the Cayman Islands. Lucas discusses the history, geography, and industry of the islands.

Geology

General

29 **Geology of the Cayman Islands.**
Brian Jones. In: *The Cayman Islands: natural history and biogeography.* Edited by M. A. Brunt, J. E. Davies. Dordrecht, Netherlands: Kluwer Academic, 1994, p. 13-49. (Monographiae Biologicae, vol. 71).

This overview provides an up-to-date account of the geology of the Cayman Islands. Jones discusses the islands' tectonic setting and geological framework, the Bluff Group, the Brac Formation, the Cayman Formation, the Pedro Castle Formation, and the Ironshore Formation.

30 **Some reefs and corals of Roatan (Honduras), Cayman Brac, and Little Cayman.**
Douglas P. Fenner. *Atoll Research Bulletin*, no. 388 (Jan. 1993), p. 1-30.

Fenner has studied the topography, zonation and coral communities of small sections of reefs in order to compare them with other well-studied Caribbean reefs. The article is divided into two major sections. In the first section, Fenner describes the reefs of northwest Roatan. In the second section, he reports on the reef profiles and coral populations of small sections of southwest Cayman Brac and northwest Little Cayman. Fenner concludes that the number and diversity of the coral present on the reefs is within the range reported for other western Caribbean reefs.

31 **Very large boulders on the coast of Grand Cayman: the effects of giant waves on rocky coastlines.**
Brian Jones, Ian G. Hunter. *Journal of Coastal Research*, vol. 8, no. 4 (Fall 1992), p. 763-74.
Large boulders, some weighing up to 40 tonnes, have been found along two stretches of rocky coastline on Grand Cayman. An analysis of the boulders, some of which are located up to 100 metres inland, indicates that they have been transported to their present site by a giant wave that swept across the island approximately 330 years ago.

32 **Void-filling deposits in karst terrains of isolated oceanic islands: a case study from Tertiary carbonates of the Cayman Islands.**
Brian Jones. *Sedimentology*, vol. 39, no. 5 (Oct. 1992), p. 857-76.
Jones provides a comprehensive view of how void-filling deposits (sediments and precipitates in caves, fossil mouldic cavities, sinkholes, joints, etc.) are generated on oceanic islands that have undergone multiple periods of karst development. The deposits described are derived from marine and terrestrial environs, mineral aerosols and groundwater. They are transported by oceanic storm waves, rain runoff, wind and groundwater. Helpful diagrams are used to illustrate void-filling deposits.

33 **Application of image analysis for delineating modern carbonate facies changes through time: Grand Cayman, western Caribbean Sea.**
Boonrasri Tongpenyai, Brian Jones. *Marine Geology*, vol. 96 (1991), p. 85-101.
This paper verifies the use of image analysis of aerial photographs for the delineation of facies in shallow lagoons; quantitatively compares different lagoons; and examines facies changes of various lagoons from 1971 to 1985.

34 **Genesis of terrestrial oncoids, Cayman Islands, British West Indies.**
Brian Jones. *Canadian Journal of Earth Sciences*, vol. 28, no. 3 (March 1991), p. 382-97.
Terrestrial oncoids are laminated, microbially formed structures which occur in vadose settings, and are formed at the atmosphere-soil or sediment or rock interface or within soil profiles. In this paper, Jones examines the occurrence, morphology, composition and microbial community of terrestrial oncoids.

35 **Pleistocene paleogeography and sea levels on the Cayman Islands, British West Indies.**
Brian Jones, Ian G. Hunter. *Coral Reefs*, vol. 9, no. 2 (1990), p. 81-91.
The authors provide a detailed examination of the paleogeography of the Cayman Islands during the Pleistocene era. They conclude that the Ironshore Formation was deposited in a large lagoon which covered the central and western part of Grand Cayman and that these lagoonal sediments were overlain by limestone. They also conclude that 125,000 years ago the sea level was six metres higher than current levels.

36 **Calcite rafts, peloids, and micrite in cave deposits from Cayman Brac, British West Indies.**
Brian Jones. *Canadian Journal of Earth Sciences*, vol. 26, no. 4 (April 1989), p. 654-64.

In this paper, Jones describes calcite rafts (thin crusts of calcite which float freely on cave ponds), comments on the formation of these calcite rafts, describes the cements and sediments that occur in the interraft cavities, and examines the origins of the peloids and micrites that are associated with calcite rafts.

37 **Formation of peloids in plant rootlets, Grand Cayman, British West Indies.**
Brian Jones, Cheryl A. Squair. *Journal of Sedimentary Petrology*, vol. 59, no. 6 (Nov. 1989), p. 1002-07.

The authors describe the peloids, a form of mud, that occur in rootlets and discuss the origins of these peloids. They also compare the peloids with those documented in the literature and comment on their environmental significance.

38 **Micro-organisms and crystal fabrics in cave pisoliths from Grand Cayman, British West Indies.**
Brian Jones, Robert W. MacDonald. *Journal of Sedimentary Petrology*, vol. 59, no. 3 (May 1989), p. 387-96.

Cave pisoliths are coated grains of sediment. The examples from Grand Cayman described in this article are formed of a nucleus surrounded by a laminae of micrite, dendrite calcite crystals and trigonal calcite crystals. This paper focuses on the role of both micro-organisms and a variety of crystals in the formation of micrite laminae.

39 **Anatomy and diagenesis of a Pleistocene carbonate breccia formed by the collapse of a seacliff, Cayman Brac, British West Indies.**
Brian Jones, Kwok-Choi Samuel Ng. *Bulletin of Canadian Petroleum Geology*, vol. 36, no. 1 (March 1988), p. 9-24.

This paper examines a breccia body which was formed by the collapse of the seacliffs on Cayman Brac approximately 125,000 years ago due to severe undercutting which was associated with wave action. The site provides an excellent opportunity to examine breccia formed in this manner.

40 **Open and filled karst features on the Cayman Islands: implications for the recognition of paleokarst.**
Brian Jones, Duncan S. Smith. *Canadian Journal of Earth Sciences*, vol. 25, no. 8 (Aug. 1988), p. 1277-91.

Jones and Smith discuss the elements of surficial, interface and subsurface karsts, document buried karst features and outline some of the criteria that might be of use in the identification of paleokarst.

41   **The structure and diagenesis of rhizoliths from Cayman Brac, British West Indies.**
Brian Jones, Kwok-Choi Samuel Ng. *Journal of Sedimentary Petrology*, vol. 58, no. 3 (May 1988), p. 457-67.
In this paper, the authors describe the morphology and the associated cements of rhizoliths from the Pleistocene limestones, and compare those cements with similar cements recorded in the literature. They also discuss the role that plant roots and their associated biota have on carbonate diagenesis.

42   **The alteration of sparry calcite crystals in a vadose setting, Grand Cayman Island.**
Brian Jones. *Canadian Journal of Earth Sciences*, vol. 24, no. 11 (Nov. 1987), p. 2292-304.
Jones examines the manner in which natural calcite cements are modified by processes operating in vadose diagenetic settings, discusses the complexity of these processes, and emphasizes the need for investigating the textures of calcite crystals at higher magnifications than are available on petrographic microscopes. His studies conclude that calcite crystals under investigation have been subjected to complex physiochemical and biochemical processes.

43   **Biogenic structures and micrite in stalactites from Grand Cayman Island, British West Indies.**
Brian Jones, A. Motyka. *Canadian Journal of Earth Sciences*, vol. 24, no. 7 (July 1987), p. 1402-11.
The authors document the occurrence of calcified filaments and bacteria-like structures in stalactites from Grand Cayman Island, and evaluate and speculate on the role such organisms might play in the formation of the stalactites. They conclude that micrite, which contains abundant amounts of bacteria-like bodies and calcified filaments, is a common component of many of the stalactites, and that algae has served to trap and bind micrite into the structure of the stalactites.

44   **Dendritic calcite crystals formed by calcification of algal filaments in a vadose environment.**
Brian Jones, C. F. Kahle. *Journal of Sedimentary Petrology*, vol. 56, no. 2 (March 1986), p. 217-27.
Using examples from the Cayman Islands, Jones and Kahle describe and discuss dendritic calcite crystals, the conditions and processes responsible for their formation, their relevance to calcified algal filaments, and the subaerial environment in which they are formed. The authors conclude that calcified algal filaments are common in vadose settings and may play an important role in the cementation processes associated with karst breccia.

45   **Marine erosion rates and coastal morphology of reef limestones on Grand Cayman Island, West Indies.**
Tom Spencer. *Coral Reefs*, vol. 4, no. 2 (Sept. 1985), p. 59-70.
Spencer reports on shoreline erosion on Grand Cayman Island which has been caused by wave and tidal action.

46 **Oncolites from a shallow lagoon, Grand Cayman Island.**
Brian Jones, Q. H. Goodbody. *Bulletin of Canadian Petroleum Geology*, vol. 33, no. 2 (June 1985), p. 254-60.

An oncolite or oncoid is a type of coated grain that has a nucleus surrounded by well-defined concentric laminations of micrite. This paper describes oncolites from a shallow lagoon on the south coast of Grand Cayman Island which do not fit this general concept. They are composed of an amalgamation of fine to coarse sand-sized skeletal fragments, lack a nucleus and have only very vaguely-defined laminations. The authors conclude that they have been formed through the action of algal filaments and mucilage sheaths binding the grains together.

47 **Substrate destruction and sediment production by the boring sponge *Cliona caribbaea* on Grand Cayman Island.**
Kelly Lee Acker, Michael J. Risk. *Journal of Sedimentary Petrology*, vol. 55, no. 5 (Sept. 1985), p. 705-11.

Cliona caribbaea occurs in shallow terraces around Grand Cayman Island as brown sheets covering and growing over both live corals and hard substrate. The authors describe the geological effect of a boring sponge on a shallow subtidal environment. The substrate removing and coral-killing activities of this sponge are so widespread and so rapid that this organism is a significant geological agent and sediment producer.

48 **Biological alteration of beachrock on Grand Cayman Island, British West Indies.**
Brian Jones, Q. H. Goodbody. *Bulletin of Canadian Petroleum Geology*, vol. 32, no. 2 (June 1984), p. 201-15.

Beachrock is subject to bioerosion by organisms such as pelecypods, worms, sponges, algae and fungi and it is thus transformed into a rock of organically secreted material. This paper outlines the role each organism plays in the transformation of the beachrock.

49 **Coastal morphology and Late Quaternary history, Cayman Islands, West Indies.**
Colin D. Woodroffe, D. R. Stoddart, R. S. Harmon, Tom Spencer. *Quaternary Research*, vol. 19 (1983), p. 64-84.

This paper examines the Pleistocene sea-level features of the Cayman Islands. The authors discuss the geology of the islands, the Pleistocene raised reef, erosional sea-level features and reef-front terraces. They conclude that the islands occur as fault blocks and that each island may have had an individual tectonic history.

50 **Shelf margin reef morphology: a clue to major off-shore sediment transport routes, Grand Cayman Island, West Indies.**
Harry Heil Roberts. *Atoll Research Bulletin*, no. 263 (Sept. 1983), p. 1-21.

Roberts' studies show that areas of sediment accumulation are also sites of sediment transport and that this is linked to reef morphology. Abundant sediments have accumulated in the deep fore-reef shelf on the northwest and southwest areas of Grand Cayman.

51 **Geomorphology and development of mangrove swamps, Grand Cayman Island, West Indies.**
Colin D. Woodroffe. *Bulletin of Marine Science*, vol. 32, no. 2 (1982), p. 381-98.
Woodroffe examines in detail the stratigraphy and subsurface topology of two areas, Barkers Peninsula and West Bay Peninsula, and proposes a model for their development. He shows that not only has the relationship between the level of the land and the sea during the Holocene submergence been a major influence on mangrove swamp geomorphology, but that both the topology of the bedrock substrate and wave and current action have also had an effect.

52 **Reefs and associated sediments of Grand Cayman Island, B.W.I.: recent carbonate sedimentation.**
Harry Heil Roberts, Robert M. Sneider. [S.l.]: Earth Enterprises, 1982. 51p. 8 maps. bibliog.
This field trip guidebook was prepared for the 1982 annual meeting of the Geological Society of America. The guidebook provides a general geologic overview. In particular, it was used to acquaint participants, prior to the four-day trip, with the processes and products that cause Holocene carbonate sediments and rocks. There are 55 black-and-white photographs, 16 graphs and 8 diagrams.

53 **Low marine terraces of Grand Cayman Island.**
K. O. Emery. *Estuarine, Coastal and Shelf Science*, vol. 12 (1981), p. 569-78.
Emery's investigations reveal six low marine terraces above the present sea level. The lowest and youngest terrace at about two metres elevation is the most widespread and represents interglacial high sea level. The higher terraces are much more eroded and no marine materials remain on them because of this erosion. This also suggests that the higher terraces are probably much older than the lower ones.

54 **Mangrove swamp stratigraphy and Holocene transgression, Grand Cayman Island, West Indies.**
Colin D. Woodroffe. *Marine Geology*, vol. 41 (1981), p. 271-94.
Woodroffe describes core contents taken in and adjacent to mangrove swamps. His studies show that the region's stratigraphy is transgressive and records Holocene submergence of the island. Radiometric dating also suggests that the island has experienced a similar sea level rise to that recorded in Florida.

55 **Micro-topographic change on calcarenites, Grand Cayman Island, West Indies.**
Tom Spencer. *Earth Surface Processes and Landforms*, vol. 6, no. 1 (Jan./Feb. 1981), p. 85-94.
Spencer's studies have monitored micro-topographic changes in limestone since little is known about erosion rates on limestone or about how such a complex terrain has been and is being produced. Data were gathered using a traversing model of the micro-erosion meter.

56 **Geology and geomorphology of Little Cayman.**
D. R. Stoddart. *Atoll Research Bulletin*, no. 241 (March 1980), p. 11-16.

This examination of rocks and landforms focuses primarily on a discussion of the Bluff Limestone and the Ironshore Formation of Little Cayman. The article is followed by three unnumbered pages of charts and graphs and ten unnumbered pages containing twenty black-and-white plates.

57 **Mangrove sediments of Little Cayman.**
Colin D. Woodroffe. *Atoll Research Bulletin*, no. 241 (March 1980), p. 17-22.

The author examines in detail the morphology of three peat substrates from mangrove areas obtained from a series of core samples. The peat substrates contain a sedimentary record of mangrove area development and indicate changes in the environment.

58 **Pleistocene patch reefs and Holocene swamp morphology, Grand Cayman Island, West Indies.**
Colin D. Woodroffe, D. R. Stoddart, Marco Enrico Clifton Giglioli. *Journal of Biogeography*, vol. 7, no. 2 (June 1980), p. 103-13.

The authors examine the relation between patterns of mangrove swamp mosaics and the substrate topology and geology of Grand Cayman. They provide descriptions of the vegetation, the substrate geology and mangrove swamp development.

59 **Shallow-water limestones from slope off Grand Cayman Island.**
K. O. Emery, J. D. Milliman. *Journal of Geology*, vol. 88, no. 4 (1980), p. 483-88.

Through these studies of shallow-water limestones, the authors conclude that the Cayman Trough was formed during the Miocene age as a climax to tectonism that began much earlier.

60 **The zonation of rocky littoral areas around Little Cayman.**
G. W. Potts. *Atoll Research Bulletin*, no. 241 (March 1980), p. 23-42.

Potts examined the distribution of rocky littoral fauna in eight sites around Little Cayman. He concludes that the molluscan species composition, the species morphology and the vertical distribution were all affected by the exposure of the individual sites. Potts describes each site and gives an indication of the species found at each site. The article is followed by nine unnumbered pages of charts and graphs and seven unnumbered pages which contain fifteen black-and-white plates.

61 **Field guidebook to the reefs and geology of Grand Cayman Island, B.W.I.**
Harry Heil Roberts. Miami Beach, Florida: Atlantic Reef Committee, University of Miami, 1977. 41p. 4 maps. bibliog.

This guidebook was prepared for the 3rd International Symposium on Coral Reefs to assist in the study of a spatially coherent group of carbonate environments. It contains information on boulder ramparts, intertidal carbonate cementation, Pleistocene carbonates, phytokarst and carbonate crusts. Roberts has included 36 black-and-white plates.

62 **Carbonate sedimentation in a reef-enclosed lagoon, North Sound, Grand Cayman Island.**
Harry Heil Roberts. *Brigham Young University Geology Studies. Special Publication*, no. 4 (April 1976), p. 97-122.
This paper assesses selected mineralogical, chemical and petrographic surface sediment parameters within the shallow marine environments of North Sound. This project was part of a study of the shallow-water sediments and ecology of reef environments associated with Grand Cayman. Also included in the paper are 6 maps, 10 tables, 5 black-and-white plates and 4 diagrams.

63 **Geology, reefs, and marine communities of Grand Cayman Island, British West Indies.**
J. Keith Rigby, Harry Heil Roberts. *Brigham Young University Geology Studies. Special Publication*, no. 4 (April 1976), p. 1-95.
This is an excellent study of Grand Cayman reef and marine communities. The report includes 1 map, 19 black-and-white plates, 4 colour plates, 15 photographs with text, 8 graphs and 5 diagrams.

64 **Black phytokarst from Hell, Cayman Islands, British West Indies.**
Robert L. Folk, Harry Heil Roberts, Clyde H. Moore. *Geological Society of America Bulletin*, vol. 84, no. 7 (July 1973), p. 2351-60.
Phytokarst is a distinctive landform resulting from algae boring into limestone. This action produces black-coated, jagged pinnacles marked by delicate, lacy dissections. Phytokarst lacks any gravitational orientation. This article contains information on phytokarst in the Cayman Islands, examines the distinction between phytokarst and other kinds of limestone, discusses the characteristics of black phytokarst and makes a comment on white phytokarst.

65 **Geophysical reconnaissance of the western Cayman Ridge.**
Peter E. Malin, William P. Dillon. *Journal of Geophysical Research*, vol. 78, no. 32 (1973), p. 7769-75.
This article supplements existing data on the Cayman Ridge and is part of a larger study conducted by the U. S. Geophysical Survey on the Yucatan continental margin. Magnetic, gravity and seismic reflection profiles indicate that the ridge is composed of sedimentary rocks overlying a magnetic foundation.

66 **Intertidal carbonate cementation Grand Cayman, West Indies.**
Clyde H. Moore, Jr. *Journal of Sedimentary Petrology*, vol. 43, no. 3 (Sept. 1973), p. 591-602.
Moore's study was undertaken to shed some light on the complexities of the processes of carbonate origins in mixed water intertidal zones.

67 **The Pleistocene rocks of the Cayman Islands.**
M. A. Brunt, Marco Enrico Clifton Giglioli, J. D. Mather, D. J. W.
Piper, Horace G. Richards. *Geological Magazine*, vol. 110, no. 3 (July
1973), p. 209-21.
This paper describes both the geology and fauna of bluff limestone formation and
Ironshore Formation communities. A table of molluscan fauna and their locations is
appended to the article.

68 **Beachrock cements, Grand Cayman Island, B.W.I.**
Clyde H. Moore, Jr. In: *Carbonate cements.* Edited by Owen P.
Bricker. Baltimore, Maryland: Johns Hopkins University Press, 1971,
p. 9-12. (The Johns Hopkins University, Studies in Geology, no. 19).
This short article describes the grain and cement types that constitute Grand Cayman
beachrock cement. There are 12 black-and-white photographs.

69 **Fault-block origin of the western Cayman Ridge, Caribbean Sea.**
Davis A. Fahlquist, David K. Davies. *Deep-Sea Research and
Oceanographic Abstracts*, vol. 18, no. 2 (Feb. 1971), p. 243-53.
This study shows that the western end of the Cayman Ridge is a fault block uplifted
some 1500 metres above the Yucatan Abyssal Plain to the north and the Bartlett
Trough to the south. The authors also suggest that the steep gradient to the north is
caused by an igneous intrusion within the block, emplaced prior to or during faulting.

70 **Mineralogical variation in lagoonal carbonates from North Sound,
Grand Cayman Island (British West Indies).**
Harry Heil Roberts. *Sedimentary Geology*, vol. 6 (1971), p. 201-13.
Roberts indicates the magnitude of change in mineralogy within the North Sound
basin of carbonate deposition and offers some general explanations for those changes.

71 **Recently cemented aggregates (grape stones), Grand Cayman
Island, B.W.I.**
Harry Heil Roberts, Clyde H. Moore, Jr. In: *Carbonate cements.*
Edited by Owen P. Bricker. Baltimore, Maryland: Johns Hopkins
University Press, 1971, p. 88-90. (The Johns Hopkins University,
Studies in Geology, no. 19).
One page of text describes grape stone, an aggregate of biogenic grains cemented by
aragonite. One map and six black-and-white photographs are included.

72 **Occurrence of aluminous lateritic soils (bauxites) in the Bahamas
and Cayman Islands.**
N. Ahmad, Robert L. Jones. *Economic Geology*, vol. 64, no. 7 (Nov.
1969), p. 804-08.
Deposits resembling Jamaican bauxite were found on Grand Cayman and at three
Bahamian sites. The authors conducted mineralogical and chemical analyses but found
that the deposits were comparable with Jamaican bauxite in neither quality nor

quantity. The deposits are of doubtful commercial value. The authors have included tables which compare the Caymanian and Bahamian samples with Jamaican samples.

73 **Recently cemented aggregates (grapestones), Grand Cayman Island, B.W.I.**
Harry Heil Roberts. *Coastal Studies Bulletin*, no. 3 (April 1969), p. 17-21.
Based on investigations of the reefs and reef-associated environments of Grand Cayman conducted in 1967, this paper describes the characteristics and distribution of recently cemented aggregates. The investigations show that localized areas of active submarine cementation have resulted in the formation of the aggregate grains. Two basic cement types are discussed: a fine-grain dark brown variety and a clear acicular variety.

74 **The Pleistocene mollusks of Grand Cayman Island, with notes of the geology of the island.**
Harald A. Rehder. *Journal of Paleontology*, vol. 36, no. 3 (May 1962), p. 583-85.
Rehder reviews current knowledge of the geology of Grand Cayman Island and presents an annotated list of fifty species of marine molluscs.

75 **The geological history of the Cayman Islands.**
Horace G. Richards. *Notulae Naturae*, no. 284 (Dec. 14, 1955), p. 1-11.
Richards describes several possible theories for the origins of the Cayman Islands: block faulting; continental drift; slip faulting; and a possible land bridge. He also speculates on how various flora and fauna arrived on the islands and gives a short commentary on land snails.

76 **Land forms of Grand Cayman Island, British West Indies.**
Edwin Beal Doran, Jr. *Texas Journal of Science*, vol. 6, no. 4 (Dec. 1954), p. 360-77.
Doran's observations were made in 1949 during field work for his dissertation on the geography of the Cayman Islands. In this article, he investigates the island's paleogeography and its geomorphic history, and comments on offshore, shore and interior land forms. In summary, he describes the island as a low, flat island which is reef-encircled with a low, cliffed, karstic shoreline except for a three mile beach in the west end. The irregularities of its surface are due to ridges produced by wave action. The accretion of successive ridges has formed the skeleton of the island.

77 **The geology of the Cayman Islands (British West Indies), and their relation to the Bartlett Trough.**
Charles Alfred Matley. *Quarterly Journal of the Geological Society of London*, vol. 82 (1926), p. 352-87.
This report is based on an eleven-day survey conducted in 1924 for the Caymanian government. Matley provides an introduction and geological description along with discussions of two underwater geological formations; the Cayman Ridge and the

Bartlett Trough. His study concludes that a narrow coastal shelf surrounds each island and that each island consists of a fault-block of white limestone from the Middle Oligocene age in Cayman Brac and from the Miocene age in the other islands. There are five maps.

78 **Species of *Lepidocyclina* and *Carpenteria* from the Cayman Islands, and their geological significance.**
Thomas Wayland Vaughan. *Quarterly Journal of the Geological Society of London*, vol. 82 (1926), p. 388-400.
Vaughan discusses and describes six examples of *Lepidocyclina* and one example of *Carpenteria*. There are three black-and-white plates.

Hydrogeology

79 **Ground water of the Cayman Islands.**
Kwok-Choi Samuel Ng, Richard G. B. Beswick. In: *The Cayman Islands: natural history and biogeography.* Edited by M. A. Brunt, J. E. Davies. Dordrecht, Netherlands: Kluwer Academic Publishers, 1994, p. 61-74. (Monographiae Biologicae, vol. 71).
In this article, the authors summarize the hydrogeological conditions, the ground water composition and the available hydrological data, and highlight the need for careful planning in exploiting this valuable but vulnerable resource. Most of the data is from Grand Cayman and Cayman Brac.

80 **Hydrogeology of Grand Cayman, British West Indies: a karstic dolostone aquifer.**
Kwok-Choi Samuel Ng, Brian Jones, Richard G. B. Beswick. *Journal of Hydrology*, vol. 134 (1992), p. 273-95.
This paper documents the hydrological characteristics of the aquifer, highlights the effects of the paleohydrological regime on the present-day groundwater system and emphasizes the geology of groundwater occurrences on Grand Cayman.

81 **A study of freshwater lens configuration in the Cayman Islands using resistivity methods.**
Stephen Fredrick Bugg, John William Lloyd. *Quarterly Journal of Engineering Geology*, vol. 9, no. 4 (1976), p. 291-302.
The freshwater lens mentioned in the title and throughout this paper is a reference to groundwater in the form of a freshwater lens resting upon saline water. The authors initially discuss the problem of identifying the base of freshwater lenses in oceanic islands. They describe their study in the Caymans in which the lens base is defined in relation to potable water standards and mapped using surface resistivity measurements with saline profile controls in boreholes.

82   **The geology of Grand Cayman and its control over the development of lenses of potable groundwater.**
John David Mather.   *Memorias-Transactions de la VI Conferencia Geologica del Caribe* (1972), p. 154-57.
Mather discusses the properties of the different rock types which are found on Grand Cayman and how these differences control the permeability of the limestone aquifer and hence the distribution of the lenses of fresh water. He found that, for the most part, the Ironshore Formation and the Bluff Limestone provided the best possibilities for fresh water lenses, while the mangrove swamp areas yielded brackish water.

Bluff Formation

83   **Caymanite, a cavity-filling deposit in the Oligocene-Miocene Bluff Formation of the Cayman Islands.**
Brian Jones.   *Canadian Journal of Earth Sciences*, vol. 29, no. 4 (April 1992), p. 720-36.
Caymanite is a multi-coloured microcrystalline dolostone named after local craftsmen who use it for making jewellery. This paper describes and discusses caymanite's occurrence, petrography, stratigraphic setting, its relationship to other cavity-filling deposits and the mode and time of its formation. Among a number of conclusions, Jones finds that caymanite originated as a limestone and was formed during two different times in the evolution of the Bluff Formation. The deposits, which are commonly found in volcano-shaped mounds, probably resulted from storm-transported sediment.

84   **Manganese precipitates in the karst terrain of Grand Cayman, British West Indies.**
Brian Jones.   *Canadian Journal of Earth Sciences*, vol. 29 (1992), p. 1125-39.
Jones sets out two objectives in this paper: to describe and document the different types of manganese precipitates that occur in the Bluff Formation, and to speculate on the source of the manganese and the role of organisms in the precipitation of manganese. He concludes that he cannot determine the exact conditions of the formation of the manganese precipitates because they are not actively forming at the present time.

85   **Dolomitization of the Oligocene-Miocene Bluff Formation on Grand Cayman, British West Indies.**
Suzanne M. Pleydell, Brian Jones, F. J. Longstaff, H. Baadsgaard.
Canadian Journal of Earth Sciences, vol. 27, no. 8 (Aug. 1990), p. 1098-1110.
The authors examine dolomitization and the early diagenetic history of the rocks in the Bluff Formation.

86 Formation of poikilotopic calcite-dolomite fabrics in the Oligocene-Miocene Bluff Formation of Grand Cayman, British West Indies.
Brian Jones, Suzanne M. Pleydell, Kwok-Choi Samuel Ng, F. J. Longstaff. *Bulletin of Canadian Petroleum Geology*, vol. 37, no. 3 (Sept. 1989), p. 255-65.

Poikilotopic calcite-dolomite fabrics are small crystals of dolomite surrounded by large crystals of calcite. They can result from the replacement of dolomite by calcite – a process called dedolomitization. Jones and his colleagues describe and document poikilotopic calcite-dolomite fabrics and discuss the processes that led to their formation in Grand Cayman. They also compare these fabrics with similar textures documented from other sequences and comment on the validity of the terms dedolomite and dedolomitization.

87 The Oligocene-Miocene Bluff Formation on Grand Cayman.
Brian Jones, Ian G. Hunter. *Caribbean Journal of Science*, vol. 25, no. 1-2 (1989), p. 71-85.

The authors describe the two sections of the Bluff Formation: the Cayman Member (Oligocene) formed of hard, microcrystalline dolostone and the Pedro Castle Member (Miocene) formed of rubbly weathering dolostone. They discuss the disconformity, characterized by numerous borings, which separates them and the implications of this disconformity. Jones and Hunter also comment on the relationship between the Bluff Formation in the Cayman Islands and Oligocene-Miocene strata in other Caribbean islands.

88 Syntaxial overgrowths on dolomite crystals in the Bluff Formation, Grand Cayman, British West Indies.
Brian Jones. *Journal of Sedimentary Petrology*, vol. 59, no. 5 (Sept. 1989), p. 839-47.

Syntaxial overgrowths on calcite are well documented but similar overgrowths on dolomite are not. Jones's analysis is important because it provides information about three-dimensional development, dolomite crystals and crystal growth.

89 Boring of various faunal elements in the Oligocene-Miocene Bluff Formation of Grand Cayman, British West Indies.
Suzanne M. Pleydell, Brian Jones. *Journal of Paleontology*, vol. 62, no. 3 (May 1988), p. 348-67.

Bioerosion is commonly associated with rocky shorelines and modern reefs, but little attention has been paid to its role in the development of ancient reefs. The authors used borings containing natural casts from the well-preserved Ironshore Formation to compare and contrast these Oligocene-Miocene borings with those from modern settings and to determine the significance of bioerosion in this area. They were also able to describe new ichnogenera and ichnospecies.

90   **Lichen and algae: agents of biodiagenesis in karst breccia from Grand Cayman Island.**
Brian Jones, C. F. Kahle.   *Bulletin of Canadian Petroleum Geology*, vol. 33, no. 4 (Dec. 1985), p. 446-61.

The authors examine the origin, significance and characteristics of the biogenic structural and textural components that occur in karst breccia which fills sinkholes, caves and fissures in the Oligocene and Miocene Bluff Formation on Grand Cayman Island.

91   **Phreatic and vadose cements in the Tertiary Bluff Formation of Grand Cayman.**
Brian Jones, E. B. Lockhart, Cheryl A. Squair.   *Bulletin of Canadian Petroleum Geology*, vol. 32, no. 4 (Dec. 1984), p. 382-97.

Cavities formed over time have been filled or partly filled with a complex sequence of dolomite and calcite cements. These cements document the passage of the rocks from the phreatic zone to the vadose zone and provide a record of highly variable pore-water chemistry.

Ironshore Formation

92   **Distribution of bivalves and gastropods in the Pleistocene Ironshore Formation, Grand Cayman, British West Indies.**
Sarah A. Cerridwen, Brian Jones.   *Caribbean Journal of Science*, vol. 27, no. 3-4 (1991), p. 97-116.

This study details the composition of the bivalve and gastropod fauna found within the Ironshore Formation and considers the distribution of that fauna in the context of Pleistocene paleogeography. The authors analyzed 32,840 shells from 44 locations. They found that the Ironshore Formation contains 83 species of marine bivalves and 90 species of marine gastropods.

93   **Tunicate spicules and their syntaxial overgrowths: examples from the Pleistocene Ironshore Formation, Grand Cayman, British West Indies.**
Brian Jones.   *Canadian Journal of Earth Sciences*, vol. 27, no. 4 (April 1990), p. 525-32.

Tunicates or ascidians (phylum Chordata), with abundant spicules or spikes near their surface, are soft-bellied animals which attach themselves to algae and sea grass. There are few descriptions of these spicules in modern carbonate sediments or ancient limestones. Jones has examined the Ironshore Formation limestones which contain diverse, well-preserved fauna that includes numerous fossil tunicate spicules. He describes them and compares them with modern tunicate spicules.

94 **The role of micro-organisms in phytokarst development on dolostones and limestones, Grand Cayman, British West Indies.**
Brian Jones. *Canadian Journal of Earth Sciences*, vol. 26, no. 11 (Nov. 1989), p. 2204-13.

An examination of numerous samples of dolostones and limestones shows that algae, fungi and bacteria play an important role in weathering. Jones describes the micro-organisms that penetrate the rock and the micro-organisms that occur in the organic coatings that cover most exposed rock surfaces. He then compares the roles of these micro-organisms in surface weathering. Jones also examines the role of micro-organisms in the surface breakdown of limestones and dolostones and looks at weathering of the Ironshore Formation by micro-organisms.

95 **Sedimentology and ichnology of a Pleistocene unconformity-bounded, shallowing-upward carbonate sequence: the Ironshore Formation, Salt Creek, Grand Cayman.**
Brian Jones, S. George Pemberton. *Palaios*, vol. 4, no. 4 (Aug. 1989), p. 343-55.

Jones and Pemberton use lithological and ichnological data to provide insights into a single carbonate sequence bounded by unconformities. They also give a detailed analysis of ichnofossils in order to show changes in environmental conditions.

96 **Ichnology of the Pleistocene Ironshore Formation, Grand Cayman Island, British West Indies.**
S. George Pemberton, Brian Jones. *Journal of Paleontology*, vol. 62, no. 4 (July 1988), p. 495-505.

The purpose of this paper is to document the abundant and well-preserved ichnofossils that occur in Pleistocene Ironshore Formation and to examine the similarities between shallow-water autochthonous carbonate ichnofossils and their siliciclastic counterparts. The ichnofossils described were created in response to hydrodynamic conditions rather than because of the composition of the substrate.

97 **The influence of plants and micro-organisms on diagenesis in caliche: example from the Pleistocene Ironshore Formation on Cayman Brac, British West Indies.**
Brian Jones. *Bulletin of Canadian Petroleum Geology*, vol. 36, no. 2 (June 1988), p. 191-201.

Jones examines the types of borings produced by roots and the effect the substrate has had on structures produced by plant roots. He also looks at the types of micro-organisms associated with roots and the types of cements which occur in the borings. Through these studies it is possible to evaluate the role of plant roots and micro-organisms on the diagenesis of caliche and its porosity and permeability.

98   **Lithophaga borings and their influence on the diagenesis of corals in the Pleistocene Ironshore Formation of Grand Cayman Island, British West Indies.**
Brian Jones, S. George Pemberton.   *Palaios*, vol. 3 (1988), p. 3-21.
Corals have been infested by the bivalve, *Lithophaga*, which has formed borings up to 15 cm long and 4 cm in diameter. In this paper, the authors document the occurrence and abundance of *Lithophaga*; describe the size and morphology of the borings; and examine the nature of the calcareous sediments that line and fill the borings. They then use this information to discuss the influence of *Lithophaga* on the diagenetic history of the coral heads and to discuss the role of *Lithophaga* in the bioerosion of coral heads.

99   **Biological factors in the formation of quiet-water ooids.**
Brian Jones, Q. H. Goodbody.   *Bulletin of Canadian Petroleum Geology*, vol. 32, no. 2 (June 1984), p. 190-200.
The authors studied oolithic limestones in the Ironshore Formation at Salt Creek. They concluded that the pellets which form the large nuclei of the ooids they examined were produced by the burrowing shrimp *Callianassa*. These pellets then underwent early lithification due to bacteria and, like the pellets, the oolithic film around the pellet nuclei was also bacterially induced. This oolithic film occurred without the grain ever being exposed to open water. These ooids differ from the norm where ooids are typically considered to be indicative of a high-energy rather than quiet-water environment.

100   **Ironshore.**
C. P. Idyll.   *Americas*, vol. 20, no. 6 (June 1968), p. 29-36.
Idyll describes the Ironshore of Cayman Brac and its formation. Limestone was laid down in the shallow sea in the Oligocene Epoch. The sea bottom then rose until it stood above the ocean surface where it was eroded by air and sea. Over this soft limestone veneer a soft marl was deposited and hardened by air, water and chemical changes.

101   **Ironshore in some West Indian islands.**
A. S. Warthin, Jr.   *Transactions of the New York Academy of Sciences*, series 2, vol. 21, no. 8 (June 1959), p. 649-52.
Warthin gives a good description and explanation of ironshore formations. Most of the examples come from Grand Cayman although ironshore formations are also found in the Bahamas, Cuba and south Florida.

Cayman Trough

102 **SeaMARC II mapping of transform faults in the Cayman Trough, Caribbean Sea.**
Eric Rosencrantz, Paul Mann. *Geology*, vol. 19, no. 7 (July 1991), p. 690-93.

This study was conducted during July and August 1989 to map the sea-floor topography and structure of the southern wall of the Cayman Trough between Honduras and Jamaica. The paper describes the location, orientation and major structure of the faults which were found. Also, the authors briefly address the tectonic implications of these faults.

103 **Age and spreading history of the Cayman Trough as determined from depth, heat flow, and magnetic anomalies.**
Eric Rosencrantz, Malcolm I. Ross, John G. Sclater. *Journal of Geophysical Research*, vol. 93, no. B3 (March 10, 1988), p. 2141-57.

The Cayman Trough provides an indication of the movement of tectonic plates surrounding the Caribbean plate. Information about the Cayman Trough can be used to reconstruct the evolution of the Caribbean area. The authors have used data concerning depth, heat flow and magnetic anomalies to determine the age and spread of the Trough to assist in further evolutionary research.

104 **The geology and evolution of the Cayman Trench.**
Michael R. Perfit, Bruce C. Heezen. *Geological Society of America Bulletin*, vol. 89 (Aug. 1978), p. 1155-74.

The authors' studies were undertaken during 1971, 1972 and 1973. Their direct sampling of the earth's crust allowed them to determine the age and composition of the rocks found in the Cayman Trench and led to a new structural and evolutionary model for the region.

105 **Inversion of magnetic anomalies and sea-floor spreading in the Cayman Trough.**
Ken C. Macdonald, T. L. Holcombe. *Earth and Planetary Science Letters*, vol. 40 (1978), p. 407-14.

Macdonald and Holcombe have based their studies concerning the measurement of sea-floor spreading on magnetic anomalies rather than using data from seismicity, heat flow, topography and plate geometry. These studies have assisted in defining the relative motion between the North American and Caribbean plates and have shed some light on sea-floor spreading processes.

106 **Petrology and geochemistry of mafic rocks from the Cayman Trench: evidence for spreading.**
Michael R. Perfit. *Geology*, vol. 5, no. 2 (Feb. 1977), p. 105-10.

Perfit provides evidence for a mid-Cayman spreading centre based on the basaltic, gabbroic and ultramafic rocks dredged from the floor of the Cayman Trough.

107 **Window on the Earth's interior.**
Robert D. Ballard. *National Geographic*, vol. 150, no. 2 (Aug. 1976), p. 228-49.
Ballard reports on dives into the Cayman Trough to map, sample and study the complex rock assemblages in one of the zones of creation and movement of the oceanic crust. Coloured diagrams and photographs help to document these studies.

108 **Return to the deep: the Cayman Trough.**
Science News, vol. 108, no. 17 (Oct. 25, 1975), p. 263.
This short article describes the preparations for a deep-sea expedition to explore the Cayman Trough and investigate plate movement in the earth's crust.

109 **Evidence for sea-floor spreading in the Cayman Trough.**
T. L. Holcombe, P. R. Vogt, J. E. Matthews, R. P. Murchison. *Earth and Planetary Science Letters*, vol. 20 (1973), p. 357-71.
The authors describe the morphology and sediments of the central portion of the Cayman Trough. Their studies are based on findings from US Naval Oceanographic Office bathymetric data. The data were obtained from tracklines which ran parallel to the long axis of the trough. Previous studies used tracklines which had run across the trough.

110 **Ultrabasic rocks from the Cayman Trough, Caribbean Sea.**
David H. Eggler, Davis A. Fahlquist, W. E. Pequenat, J. M. Herndon. *Geological Society of America Bulletin*, vol. 84, no. 6 (June 1973), p. 2133-38.
The authors studied a collection of ultrabasic rocks which were dredged from the centre of the Cayman Trough in 1970. Serpentinite, which may be altered spinel herzolite, dominates the collection and is believed to be bedrock in the area dredged.

111 **Heat flow and continuous seismic profiles in the Cayman Trough and Yucatan Basin.**
A. J. Erickson, C. E. Helsey, Gene Simmons. *Geological Society of America Bulletin*, vol. 83, no. 5 (May 1972), p. 1241-60.
This paper interprets data relevant to the sedimentary and tectonic history of the western Caribbean. Seismic and bathymetric data were gathered along 2600 kilometres of the western Cayman Trough and in the Yucatan Basin. The highest heat flow values were located in the deepest areas of the trough.

112 **Magnetic anomalies and tectonics of the Cayman Trough.**
D. I. Gough, J. R. Heirtzler. *Geophysical Journal of the Royal Astronomical Society*, vol. 18 (1969), p. 33-49.
This report describes the studies which have led to a magnetic residual total-field anomaly map for the Cayman Trough, Cayman Ridge and part of the Nicaragua Rise.

113 **Geophysical study of the Cayman Trough.**
Carl O. Bowin. *Journal of Geophysical Research*, vol. 73, no. 16
(Aug. 15, 1968), p. 5159-73.

Bowin investigated the age and history of the Cayman Trough in 1965 using
continuous bathymetric, gravity and magnetic measurements. Although age and
history could not be clearly defined, Bowin does conclude that the Trough is growing
eastward. However, its slow growth rate and lack of characteristic central magnetic
anomalies suggest that the Trough probably resulted from processes different from
those which produced the world rift system.

Oceanography

114 **Cayman Islands natural resources study: results of the
investigations into the physical oceanography.**
J. Darbyshire, I. Bellamy, Brian Jones.   London: Ministry of Overseas
Development, 1976. 121p. 30 maps. (Cayman Islands Natural
Resources Study, part III).
The third volume of the *Cayman Islands natural resources study* (q.v.) was prepared
under the following terms of reference: to establish baseline oceanographic data; to
determine the physical parameters upon which the effects of dredging and the
resultant turbidity are dependent; to assess the type of sand found in the marine
environment and its suitability for building purposes; to recommend areas suitable for
sand extraction; and to advise on safeguards.

115 **Physical processes in a fringing reef system.**
Harry Heil Roberts, Stephen P. Murray, Joseph N. Suhayda.   *Journal
of Marine Research*, vol. 33, no. 2 (1975), p. 233-60.
The purpose of this paper is to present the results of field and laboratory studies which
were designed to measure the magnitude of the effects of waves and currents which
interact with Caribbean reef systems. The studies were undertaken on Grand Cayman
during November and December 1972 with supporting research conducted in
Barbados in 1973. The studies showed that deepwater wave characteristics were
significantly modified by reef morphology, leading the researchers to conclude that
there is strong interaction between currents and reef systems.

116 **On the upper layer circulation in the Cayman Sea.**
Ingvar Emilsson. In: *Symposium on investigations and resources of the
Caribbean Sea and adjacent regions.*   Paris: Unesco, 1971, p. 53-60.
This paper details the main features of water circulation in the upper 500 metres of the
Cayman Sea and, in particular, the layer that extends from the surface down to the
intermediate salinity maximum, around 200 metres. Emilsson also discusses the main
factors that influence water movement and the role played by the Cayman Sea in the

general circulation in the Central American seas. These proceedings contain 65 papers on physical and chemical oceanography, marine geology and geophysics and marine biology presented at the symposium held at Willemstad, Curacao in November 1968.

117 Precise temperature measurements in the Cayman Trench.
A. E. Gilmour. *Deep-Sea Research*, vol. 16 (April 1969), p. 197-203.

The author describes measurements made on a north-south section across the Cayman Trench using a precise bathythermograph with quartz crystal temperature sensors.

118 A contribution to the hydrography of the Caribbean and Cayman Seas.
Albert Eide Parr. *Bulletin of the Bingham Oceanographic Collection*, vol. 5, no. 4 (1937), p. 1-110.

This is the first report of the hydrographic investigations of the Central American seas begun by the Yale Oceanographic Expedition to the Gulf of Mexico in 1932.

Travel Guides

119 **The Berlitz travellers Caribbean.**
New York: Berlitz, 1992-. annual. (The Berlitz Travellers Guide).
Primarily, this is a directory of accommodation, but there is also some information outlining the cultural significance of the individual island nations and a commentary on their individual characteristics.

120 **Best dives of the Caribbean.**
Joyce Huber, Jon Huber. Edison, New Jersey: Hunter Publishing, 1994. 342p. 55 maps.
The authors provide detailed reports on reefs, wrecks and marine parks; dive resorts, hotels, inns and villas; dive operations; sailing and yachting vacations; and sightseeing. Each dive site is rated with one to five stars, and maps indicate the location of each site. In the Cayman Islands section (p. 111-30), the Hubers list nine dive sites for Grand Cayman and two each for Cayman Brac and Little Cayman. They also list two snorkelling sites off Grand Cayman, one off Cayman Brac and seven off Little Cayman.

121 **The Caribbean and the Bahamas.**
James Henderson. London: Cadogan Books, 1994. 3rd ed.
764p. 40 maps. (Cadogan Guides).
In this readable, concise guide, Henderson provides information about the Lesser Antilles, the Greater Antilles and the Bahamas. The Cayman Islands are included under the Greater Antilles. He includes information about transport, currency, diving, beaches, sports, festivals, accommodation and dining.

122 **Depth perception.**
Samuel Young. *Travel Holiday*, vol. 177 (Feb. 1994), p. 46-53, 86, 92-93.

Young comments on diving and snorkelling and includes excellent underwater photographs by David Doubilet. There is a separate section (p. 53) entitled 'Island Amenities' which offers information about transport, accommodation and restaurants.

123 **Diving and snorkeling guide to the Cayman Islands: Grand Cayman, Little Cayman, and Cayman Brac.**
Carl Roessler. Houston, Texas: Pisces Books, 1993. 2nd ed. 92p. 3 maps. bibliog. (Diving and Snorkeling Guides Series).

Roessler gives detailed descriptions of 30 dive sites off Grand Cayman and four dive sites off Little Cayman and Cayman Brac. For each site, he discusses the depth range, the strength of the currents, the expertise required, accessibility to the site and the type of marine life one can expect to encounter. There is also information concerning travel, customs and immigration, dining and shopping and diving safety.

124 **A field trip underwater with the renowned 'shark lady'.**
Judith W. Shanks. *Sea Frontiers*, vol. 39 (Nov.-Dec. 1993), p. 40-43.

The 'shark lady' is Eugenie Clark, a senior research scientist in zoology at the University of Maryland. Shanks signed on with her to help research sand tilefish (Malacanthus plumieri) off Cayman Brac. The author describes the work they undertook and provides information about diving and study opportunities in the Cayman Islands.

125 **Fodor's affordable Caribbean.**
New York: Fodor's Travel Publications, 1993-. annual. (Fodor's Affordables).

This Fodor's publication is written for people who are travelling on a limited budget. The format is very similar to other Fodor travel guides (q.v.). Included in the book are sections on beaches, sports, shopping, dining, accommodation and night life.

126 **Undiscovered islands of the Caribbean.**
Burl Willes. Santa Fe, New Mexico: John Muir Publications, 1992. 3rd ed. 276p. 29 maps.

In the section on Little Cayman and Cayman Brac (p. 245-56), Willes offers information on accommodation and diving. (He does not mention Grand Cayman.) This guide also covers the lesser known islands of the Bahamas, Puerto Rico, the Leeward Islands, the Grenadines, Venezuela, Belize, the West Caribbean and the British Virgin Islands.

127 **Birnbaum's Caribbean.**
New York: Harper Perennial, 1991-. annual. (A Stephen Birnbaum Travel Guide).

This useful guide covers transport, shopping, sports, accommodation and dining. This volume continues, in part, *Birnbaum's Caribbean, Bermuda and the Bahamas* which began publication in 1985.

128 **Frommer's comprehensive travel guide. Caribbean.**
Darwin Porter, Danforth Prince. New York: Prentice-Hall,
1991-. annual.

Frommer's comprehensive travel guide. Caribbean (the title *Frommer's Caribbean*
appears on the spine) provides information about accommodation, dining, sports and
recreation, shopping and sightseeing. This publication was originally entitled *Arthur
Frommer's dollarwise guide to the Caribbean, including Bermuda and the Bahamas*.
It eventually became *Frommer's dollarwise guide to the Caribbean* in 1986 when
Bermuda and the Bahamas were given their own guide. In 1990, it became *Frommer's
Caribbean* with the current title change the following year.

129 **Cayman diver's guide.**
Shlomo Cohen. Tel Aviv: Seapen Books, 1990. 191p. 54 maps.

Cohen lists 74 dive sites around Grand Cayman and provides a detailed description
and map for 39 of them. Similarly, he lists 30 sites around Cayman Brac and 24 sites
around Little Cayman, and then describes six sites in detail for each island. Some of
the dive site descriptions include diagrams indicating both the surface and the
underwater marinescape and suggested diving routes. There is also a fish index, a
diving company directory and a section on underwater photography.

130 **The Caribbean islands handbook.**
Bath, England: Trade & Travel Publications, 1989-. annual.

This tourist guide is aimed at the independent traveller who wishes to explore all
aspects of island life and culture. The editors include information on history and
government, the economy, fauna and flora, diving and marine life, beaches and water
sports and festivals. Separate sections for each of the three islands give information
about accommodation and dining. A further section outlines important visitor
information, including necessary documents, transport and communication, currency,
health matters and climate.

131 **Tropical shipwrecks: a vacationing diver's guide to the Bahamas
and Caribbean.**
Daniel Berg, Denise Berg. East Rockaway, New York: Aqua
Explorers, Inc., 1989. 150p. 2 maps. bibliog.

The authors describe three shipwrecks off Cayman Brac (p. 62-64), nine off Grand
Cayman (p. 69-83), and one off Little Cayman (p. 94-96). For each site, the authors
provide information on the depth of the wreck, the ocean currents, visibility and the
types of aquatic life to be seen. The Bergs also list wrecks off the coasts of the
Bahamas, Barbados, the Bay Islands, Belize, the British Leeward and Windward
Islands, the French West Indies, Jamaica, Mexico, the Netherlands Antilles, Puerto
Rico, the Turks and Caicos Islands and the U. S. Virgin Islands. A directory of dives
is included.

132 Bon voyage: the Cayman Islands.

Jinx Morgan, Jefferson Morgan. *Bon Appetit*, vol. 33, no. 9 (Sept. 1988), p. 38, 40, 42, 44-46.

The Morgans provide information about banking, tourism, restaurants and accommodation. They have also included four Caymanian recipes: fiery deep-fried coconut shrimp, pineapple plum sauce, Cayman-style snapper stew and coconut pecan pie.

133 The Cayman Islands.

Rachel J. Christmas. *Travel-Holiday*, vol. 169 (Jan. 1988), p. 52-57.

Christmas describes scuba diving, snorkelling, submarine dives and individual dive sites. She also provides telephone numbers and prices for accommodation.

134 The Caymans.

Mechtild Hoppenrath. *Travel à la Carte*, vol. 14, no. 4 (Sept. 1988), p. 34-36.

Written for Canadian travellers, this short article focuses on diving, deep-sea fishing and the islands' hotels.

135 Cash, splash, romance – sounds of a Cayman Island vacation.

Steven Curson. *Canadian Travel Courier*, vol. 22, no. 18 (July 9, 1987), p. 10.

This short article has been written for members of Canada's travel industry. Curson gives a brief, general overview of the Cayman Islands as a tourist resort and holiday destination.

136 Caymans.

Geri Murphy. *Skin Diver*, vol. 36, no. 2 (Feb. 1987), p. 53-94.

This 42-page diving guide contains many advertisments, but it also provides information on transport to the islands, taxi and car rentals, restaurants, accommodation, entertainment, climate, geography, diving services, dive sites and marine parks.

137 Cayman Islands coral.

Heather Townshend. *Geographical Magazine*, vol. 58, no. 4 (April 1986), p. 198-201.

This brief article provides information primarily about diving in the Cayman Islands.

138 Fodor's Caribbean.

New York: Fodor's Travel Publications, 1986- . annual.

This very useful guide gives a great deal of practical information concerning accommodation, dining and shopping. There is also historical and descriptive information about the islands. This annual began publication in 1960 under the title *Fodor's guide to the Caribbean, Bahamas, and Bermuda*. It subsequently became

Fodor's Caribbean, Bahamas, and Bermuda and then in 1980, *Fodor's Caribbean and the Bahamas.* In 1986 the title was changed to *Fodor's Caribbean* when the publishers began a separate publication for the Bahamas.

139   **Submarines for everyone.**
Bill Hirsch, Yvette Cardozo.   *Oceans*, vol. 19, no. 2 (March/April 1986), p. 46-51, 57.

The authors describe submarine dives which are available for visitors to Grand Cayman. Research Submarines Ltd., conducts dives up to 800 feet deep, while Atlantis Submarines' dives are up to 80 feet deep.

140   **The Cayman Islands.**
Roger Cox.   *Travel-Holiday*, vol. 161 (May 1984), p. 72-75, 88-89.

Cox's general introduction to the Cayman Islands provides a brief history and descriptions of George Town and Grand Cayman. There is also some information about Little Cayman and Cayman Brac.

141   **Dive Cayman! a guide to reefs of the Cayman Islands.**
Nancy Sefton.   Grand Cayman: Undersea Photo Supply, 1981. 96p. 2 maps. bibliog.

Sefton describes eight snorkelling sites, 37 scuba sites and two celebrity wreck sites off the coast of Grand Cayman. She also describes several sites off Cayman Brac and Little Cayman. The book includes a section on the biology and ecology of coral reefs.

142   **Fielding's Caribbean.**
Redondo Beach, California: Fielding Worldwide, 1981- . annual. (Fielding Travel Guides).

This publication includes an introduction to the Cayman Islands and information on politics, lifestyle, medical facilities, currency, communications, accommodation and dining. Hotels and restaurants are rated on a one-to-five star system. Comments tend to be positive about everything, so this guide is often more useful as a directory than as a resource for decision-making.

143   **Cayman, underwater paradise.**
Paul Humann, Feodor Pitcairn.   Bryn Athyn, Pennsylvania: Reef Dwellers Press, 1979. 90p. map.

This book provides descriptions of individual reefs and wrecks in the waters of the Cayman Islands. There are 73 spectacular colour plates.

144   **Grand Cayman.**
Walter Wetherell.   *Travel*, vol. 146, no. 1 (July 1976), p. 32-37.

Wetherell does not see Grand Cayman as an unspoiled paradise waiting to be ruined by tourism, but rather as an island that is making a well-thought out adjustment to the 20th century. The article (p. 32-35) is followed by a section outlining weather, customs, sight-seeing, diving, accommodation and restaurants.

145 **Development in the Cayman Islands.**
Alexander Melamid. *Geographical Review*, vol. 65 (Jan. 1975),
p. 107-08.
In this short follow-up to Billmyer's 1946 article (q.v.), Melamid describes
developments in banking, telecommunications, transport and tourism.

146 **Tropical trio: new attraction.**
Alice Grant. *Oceans*, vol. 7, no. 5 (Sept./Oct. 1974), p. 36-38.
Grant provides a brief history of the three Cayman Islands along with an outline of the
development of the tourist industry. There is also information on diving,
accommodation and island life.

147 **An adventurer's guide to the unspoiled Cayman Islands, the
islands time forgot.**
George I. Hudson.   Grand Cayman: Caribbean Colour Ltd., 1973.
320p. 3 maps.
Hudson provides information on geography and geology, finance, hurricanes, shells
and molluscs, fishing, diving, flora and fauna, and hotels. There are numerous black-
and-white photographs and four poor colour plates. This work is a considerable
expansion of his 1965 booklet (q.v.).

148 **The unspoiled Cayman Islands: the islands that time forgot.**
George I. Hudson.   Grand Cayman: Caribbean Colour Ltd., 1965.
80p. 4 maps. bibliog.
Hudson touches on a number of topics in this booklet, including history, diving
and wrecks, flora, shells and shell collecting, turtles and turtle research and
accommodation.

149 **The Cayman Islands.**
James H. S. Billmyer. *Geographical Review*, vol. 36, no. 1 (Jan.
1946), 29-43.
Billmyer wrote this article as an enticement to the discerning tourist. He discusses
climate, communications, history, population, occupations and way of life, buildings,
mores and education and health. Interestingly, Billmyer presents the Cayman Islands
as an 'anthropological laboratory', a group of isolated islands offering a wealth of
material for future study. There are 2 maps and 18 black-and-white photographs.

150 **The Cayman Islands.**
A. J. A. Douglas. *Geographical Journal*, vol. 95, no. 2 (Feb. 1940),
p. 126-31.
Douglas gives a general description of the islands, including history, population,
climate, industry and health. According to the magazine's editor, Douglas' article was
published because, '[a] number of cruising liners now call during the winter at the
Cayman Islands, and it is hoped that the following notes may prove a useful
supplement to other information available.' (p. 126)

Travellers' Accounts

151 **A reporter at large: to the Miskito Bank.**
Peter Matthiessen. *The New Yorker*, vol. 43 (Oct. 28, 1967), p. 120, 122, 124, 127-28, 130, 133-34, 136, 138, 140, 143-46, 149-50, 152-164.
Matthiessen gives a general history of the Caymans and describes his trips to the islands and his adventures on a turtling voyage during the 1960s.

152 **Caribbean isle of content.**
Esther Chapman. *The Crown Colonist* (Dec. 1949), p. 766-67.
Chapman gives the reader an idyllic view of Grand Cayman, with commentary on the scenery, government, food and people.

153 **Grand Cayman – forgotten by time.**
Karl Baarslag. In: *Islands of adventure*. London: The Travel Book Club, 1944, p. 55-67.
In the book, Baarslag offers observations on a number of somewhat unknown islands and island groups throughout the world. He visited Grand Cayman briefly in 1934 and describes his impressions based on a 'passing glimpse'. Baarslag provides a good description of Grand Cayman in the mid-1930s and characterizes Caymanians as a gracious and friendly people who speak a form of 17th century English.

154 **Waters of the west.**
Kenneth Pringle. London: George Allan and Unwin, 1938. 325p.
Pringle provides gentle descriptions of a number of countries in the Caribbean region. Chapter 3, 'Grand Cayman and Belize', describes an idyllic Christmas trip to Grand Cayman (p. 180-201).

155 **Notes on 'A governor's cruise in the West Indies in 1884': being an abridgement of a narrative written by Sir H. W. Norman.**
J. P. Thomson. *Quarterly of the Royal Geographical Society of Australia*, vol. 9 (1894), p. 7-14.

This article outlines Sir Henry W. Norman's cruise in 1884. At the time, he was governor of Jamaica and, as governor, was also responsible for the Cayman Islands and the Turks and Caicos Islands. A brief history of the Cayman Islands is followed by commentary on the governor's activities while visiting all three islands in the Caymans group. Of particular note are the governor's observations on the people of the islands.

Flora and Fauna

General

156 **The Cayman Islands: natural history and biogeography.**
Edited by M. A. Brunt, J. E. Davies. Dordrecht, Netherlands: Kluwer
Academic Publishers, 1994. 604p. 7 maps. bibliog. (Monographiae
Biologicae, vol. 71).

The purpose of this volume is to consolidate scattered information into a coherent
account of the biogeography and ecology of the islands. The twenty-five articles
which make up the book are listed separately under their appropriate subjects in this
bibliography.

157 **Rare and endemic plants, animals and habitats in the Cayman
Islands, and related legislation.**
J. E. Davies. In: *The Cayman Islands: natural history and
biogeography*. Edited by M. A. Brunt, J. E. Davies. Dordrecht,
Netherlands: Kluwer Academic Publishers, 1994, p. 527-41.
(Monographiae Biologicae, vol. 71).

Davies summarizes what is known about the endemic species of the Cayman Islands
and considers some non-endemic groups which need to be taken into account in any
attempt to plan conservation methods. He also outlines important habitats and gives an
account of the present local legislation and international conventions in force
concerning conservation matters.

158 **Scientific studies in the Cayman Islands.**
J. E. Davies. In: *The Cayman Islands: natural history and biogeography.* Edited by M. A. Brunt, J. E. Davies. Dordrecht, Netherlands: Kluwer Academic Publishers, 1994, p. 1-12. (Monographiae Biologicae, vol. 71).

Davies outlines the earliest known natural history collections from 1886, 1888 and 1889. There is also a description of the first major expedition, the Oxford University Cayman Islands Biological Expedition of 1938. In addition, Davies provides information about the 1974/75 Natural Resources Study (q.v.) and the 1975 Royal Society/Cayman Islands Government expedition to Little Cayman. The results of this expedition were published in the *Atoll Research Bulletin* in 1980 (q.v.). There are also tables listing thirty-four unpublished theses which were completed between 1953 and 1992; hydrographic surveys and charts from 1817 to 1985; aerial photography maps from 1946 to 1992; and topographic mapping activities from 1965 to 1988.

159 **Creator's glory: photographs of the wildlife of Grand Cayman Island.**
Richard Ground. George Town: Dace and Richard Ground for the National Trust for the Cayman Islands, 1989. 84p.

This is not a field guide, nor is it intended to be one. Ground's photographs are meant to celebrate the diversity and beauty of the island's wildlife. There are 158 colour photographs of flowers, insects, reptiles and birds.

160 **A field guide to southeastern and Caribbean seashores: Cape Hatteras to the Gulf Coast, Florida, and the Caribbean.**
Eugene H. Kaplan. Boston, Massachusetts: Houghton Mifflin, 1988. 425p. map. bibliog. (The Peterson Field Guide Series, 36).

This work, sponsored by the National Audubon Society and the National Wildlife Federation, describes the ecology and common organisms of seashores from North Carolina to Florida, the Gulf Coast and the Caribbean. It identifies plants and animals and describes all the common seashore environments – sandy beaches, rocky shores, turtle grass beds, mangrove swamps and scrub forests. A glossary and 65 black and white and coloured plates are included.

161 **The terrestrial fauna (excluding birds and insects) of Little Cayman.**
M. V. Hounsome. *Atoll Research Bulletin*, no. 241 (March 1980), p. 81-90.

Hounsome records the eighty-one species of fauna which were found on Little Cayman but does not provide annotations or descriptions. There are two tables. One table lists all the species found with an indication of the habitat type favoured by each. The second table lists the seven habitat types which Hounsome has identified and the number of species found in each type.

162 **Biological investigations in a tropical lagoon, Grand Cayman, British West Indies.**
Geoffrey W. J. Swain, Laurence E. Hull. *Symposium on Progress in Marine Research in the Caribbean and Adjacent Regions, FAO Fisheries Report*, vol. 200 (1977), p. 449-67.

The authors report that studies of the North and Little Sounds on Grand Cayman Island reveal 98 species of marine flora and 520 species of marine fauna. Five distinct regions are also identified: the shallow sediment community, the organic sediment community, the deep lagoon community, the pre-reef plain community and the back-reef community. This article also includes tables of quantitative data and a checklist of the principle species.

163 **A guide to the natural history of the Cayman Islands.**
Nancy Sefton, ed.   Grand Cayman: Cayman Islands Conservation Association and Cayman Free Press, 1976. 80p. 2 maps.

This book contains information on the marine life, mangrove swamps and land life on the islands. It is an excellent introduction for children, but is also useful for adults. The book is well-illustrated with black-and-white photographs and pen and ink drawings. There is also a useful glossary.

164 **Heat and water balance studies on Grand Cayman.**
Shih-Ang Hsu, Marco Enrico Clifton Giglioli, J. Davies. *Caribbean Journal of Science*, vol. 12, no. 1-2 (June 1972), p. 9-22.

These studies are based on climatological data and field measurements taken between 1967 and 1970. Soil moisture content was estimated by measuring the difference between precipitation and evaporation on sandy coasts and between precipitation and evapotranspiration on mangrove swamp areas. Heat balance studies were conducted on a mangrove swamp floor. The researchers found that potential evapotranspiration can be predicted by the ratio of net radiation to latent heat of vaporization.

165 **Environments and organic communities of North Sound, Grand Cayman, B.W.I.**
Harry Heil Roberts. *Caribbean Journal of Science*, vol. 11, no. 1-2 (March-June 1971), p. 67-79.

Roberts identifies and describes eight environments and ecological zones: reef crest, rubble flat, moat, rock floor, sand flat, grass plain, restricted lagoon and shore zone. Black-and-white plates illustrate each zone except the restricted lagoon. One table of data and four maps are included.

166 **Some notes from a West Indian coral island.**
T. M. Savage English. *Royal Botanic Gardens, Kew. Bulletin of Miscellaneous Information*, no. 10 (1913), p. 367-72.

Savage English's observations are based on three years' residence in Grand Cayman. He provides information on the island's climate, flora, reptiles and insects, topography and crabs. He also speculates on how some plants may have reached the island by wind, birds, storms and the sea.

Vegetation

167 **Mangrove swamps of the Cayman Islands.**
M. A. Brunt, F. J. Burton. In: *The Cayman Islands: natural history and biogeography.* Edited by M. A. Brunt, J. E. Davies. Dordrecht, Netherlands: Kluwer Academic Publishers, 1994, p. 283-305. (Monographiae Biologicae, vol. 71).

Much of the information in this article is based on surveys undertaken between 1965 and 1976. The authors discuss mangrove swamp development in the Cayman Islands and the mangrove species which are found. They also outline the major factors affecting the mangrove swamp environment: climate and hurricanes, tides, shoreline topography, current and wave erosion, flooding and groundwater, salinity, nutrient availability and the associated fauna and soil bacteria.

168 **Phytogeography of the Cayman Islands.**
George R. Proctor. In: *The Cayman Islands: natural history and biogeography.* Edited by M. A. Brunt, J. E. Davies. Dordrecht, Netherlands: Kluwer Academic Publishers, 1994, p. 237-44. (Monographiae Biologicae, vol. 71).

In their 1984 study (q.v.), Proctor and Brunt listed 601 species of vascular plants. New studies have added another 57 species in 33 families. Proctor lists and discusses these new species. He also comments on species introduced into the islands which have now become part of the permanent flora and explores the links between Caymanian species and species found in Jamaica, Cuba and the Greater Antilles.

169 **Vegetation of the Cayman Islands.**
M. A. Brunt. In: *The Cayman Islands: natural history and biogeography.* Edited by M. A. Brunt, J. E. Davies. Dordrecht, Netherlands: Kluwer Academic Publishers, 1994, p. 245-82. (Monographiae Biologicae, vol. 71).

Following J. S. Beard's system of classifying tropical American vegetation into a series of formations, Brunt has divided Caymanian vegetation into three formations: dry evergreen formation, seasonal swamp formation and swamp formation (marine and freshwater). He describes in detail the vegetation in each type of formation and, through a variety of charts and tables, outlines the species he found and their distribution.

170 **Fruits and vegetables of the Caribbean.**
M. J. Bourne, G. W. Lennox, S. A. Seddon. London: Macmillan Caribbean, 1988. 58p.

This handy, illustrated guide identifies forty-eight of the most commonly found fruits and vegetables of the region. The authors have described each species' origin, its botanical characteristics and its uses.

171   **Caribbean wild plants and their uses.**
Penelope N. Honychurch.   London: Macmillan Caribbean, 1986.
166p. bibliog.

Honychurch describes and illustrates approximately one hundred wild plants in the Caribbean which are used as remedies for illness or which are associated with folklore. The main body of the book contains detailed information on seventy-three dicotyledons (plants having two seed leaves), twenty monocotyledons (plants having one seed leaf) and five miscellaneous plants. There are also lists of medicinal compounds and the plants in which they are found, together with a list of the plants classified under the ailments for which they may be used as the remedy. A glossary provides a list of botanical terms and there are indexes of French and patois names, English names and scientific names.

172   **Flora of the Cayman Islands.**
George R. Proctor, M. A. Brunt.   London: HMSO, 1984. 834p.
3 maps. bibliog. (Kew Bulletin Additional Series, XI).

The introduction to this full description of Caymanian flora provides background material on the islands' geographic and flora history, notes concerning species and varieties, information on environmental and plant communities, and a history of previous botanical collections. The description of the flora, 601 species altogether, is divided into two Divisions, pteridophyta and spermatophyta. The spermatophyta are divided into two Classes, gymnospermae and angiospermae, and two Subclasses, monocotyledons and dicotyledons. The authors have also provided a glossary, an index of common names and an index of botanical names. Reproduced in this volume are 3 maps, 3 black-and-white plates, 256 plant drawings, 25 diagrams and 5 tables of data.

173   **Development of mangrove swamps behind beach ridges, Grand Cayman Island, West Indies.**
Colin D. Woodroffe.   *Bulletin of Marine Science*, vol. 33, no. 4
(1983), p. 864-80.

Woodroffe examines the stratigraphy and development of mangrove swamps in two areas where the formation of beach ridges has brought about seasonal flooding caused by rainwater and not regular inundation caused by the ocean tides. He concludes that, although the early stages of development of tidal and non-tidal swamps and their vegetation are similar, their substrate characteristics do differ because of the presence or absence of tidal influence.

174   **Cayman Islands seashore vegetation: a study in comparative biogeography.**
Jonathan D. Sauer.   Berkeley, California: University of California
Press, 1982. 161p. map. bibliog. (University of California Publications
in Geography, vol. 25).

Sauer has written a detailed investigation of shoreline vegetation patterns and processes. He provides a discussion of topology and geology, climate, tides and currents and storm history. There are also chapters on the history of human intervention, vegetation dynamics and a variety of geographic comparisons. This excellent study includes 13 tables of original data, 25 vegetation profiles, 39 photographic plates and an extensive bibliography.

175 Middle world of the mangrove.

Nancy Sefton. *Sea Frontiers*, vol. 27, no. 5 (Sept./Oct. 1981), p. 267-73.

This is a vivid description of mangrove swamps and swamp life. Sefton has based her generalized observations on her extensive knowledge of Cayman mangrove areas. There are 7 colour plates.

176 Checklist of the plants of Little Cayman.

George R. Proctor. *Atoll Research Bulletin*, no. 241 (March 1980), p. 71-80.

Proctor lists 240 species from 72 plant families found on Little Cayman. There are no descriptions, no annotations and no commentary.

177 Trees of the Caribbean.

S. A. Seddon, G. W. Lennox. London: Macmillan Caribbean, 1980. 74p.

This guide has been designed as a companion to *Flowers of the Caribbean, the Bahamas, and Bermuda* (q.v.) and, as such, is for individuals with little or no botanical training. The book is divided into four sections: ornamental trees, fruit trees, coast trees and palm and palm-like trees. For each entry, the authors have provided at least one colour photograph; information regarding leaf shape, size and colour; and descriptions of the flower and fruit. Each entry also includes the botanical family name and the scientific and common names.

178 Vegetation of Little Cayman.

D. R. Stoddart. *Atoll Research Bulletin*, no. 241 (March 1980), p. 53-69.

Stoddart lists the species found in three major vegetation communities: the inland vegetation community (dry evergreen forest, dry evergreen woodland, dry evergreen thicket and evergreen brushland), the coastal vegetation community (sandy beach, cobble beach, coastal sand flats, Ironshore outcrop and steep rocky coast) and the mangrove community (coastal mangroves, mangroves of coastal ponds and sand flats, inland mangroves and herbaceous swamp). The article is followed by two unnumbered pages of maps and eight unnumbered pages which contain fifteen black-and-white plates.

179 Flowers of the Caribbean, the Bahamas, and Bermuda.

G. W. Lennox, S. A. Seddon. London: Macmillan, 1978. 72p.

This book is designed for individuals with little or no botanical background. The flora are divided into three sections: herbs and shrubs, trees, and orchids. For each of the fifty entries, the authors have provided a colour photograph; the common, local and scientific names; and a short description of the specimen. Although this handy guide does not cover all species of flowering plants, it does include the more common ones.

180   **Flowers of the Cayman Islands.**
    Judy Cunninghame.   Hollywood, Florida: Dukane Press, 1970. 1 vol.
This slight volume contains twelve watercolour plates of Caymanian flowers. There is no text.

181   **Tropical trees found in the Caribbean, South America, Central America, Mexico.**
    Dorothy Hargreaves, Bob Hargreaves.   Portland, Oregon: Hargreaves Industrial, 1965. 64p.
This booklet provides a descriptive annotation and a colour photograph for each of seventy trees found throughout the region. Each annotation gives a good description; a note on geographic distribution; and the scientific name in Latin, as well as the common name in English, Spanish, French and Dutch.

182   **Tropical blossoms of the Caribbean.**
    Dorothy Hargreaves, Bob Hargreaves.   Lahaina, Hawaii: Ross-Hargreaves, 1960. 64p.
This handbook includes entries for both flowers and trees from the Caribbean region and tropical South America. Each entry is accompanied by a colour photograph and includes the common and botanical names, as well as a description and a location. It is similar in format to the authors' *Tropical trees . . .* (q.v.).

183   **Manual of the grasses of the West Indies.**
    Albert S. Hitchcock.   Washington, DC: Government Printing Office, 1936. 439p. (US Department of Agriculture. Miscellaneous Publication, no. 243).
This is a revision of Hitchcock and Chase's 1917 publication (q.v.). Following a brief introduction to the grasses, Hitchcock gives very full and detailed descriptions, including an indication of distribution, of over 550 species. The list includes 38 new species. There are also 374 pen-and-ink drawings; at least one species of each genera is illustrated.

184   **Grasses of the West Indies.**
    Albert S. Hitchcock, Agnes Chase.   *Contributions from the United States National Herbarium*, vol. 18 (Sept. 1, 1917), p. 261-471.
This is a detailed list of the grasses from over one hundred genera. Each entry includes the scientific and common names; a description; and an indication of location and distribution. The list is based primarily on a study of the collection in the United States Herbarium. Also included is a 67 page catalogue of the National Herbarium collection arranged by collectors' names and by National Herbarium numbers.

185 **List of plants collected in the Bahamas, Jamaica and Grand Cayman.**
Albert S. Hitchcock. *Missouri Botanical Garden. Fourth Annual Report*, vol. 4 (1893), p. 47-179.

The collection was made during the winter of 1890-91. The 'Catalogue of Plants' (p. 57-157) lists a total of 953 species. Each entry is slight, giving the species name and a location or distribution. The catalogue is preceded by ten pages of introduction and a discussion concerning the classification of the species found. It also contains a chart which lists each species and its distribution. The emphasis of the supporting text is on the Bahamas.

186 **Cayman Islands.**
William Fawcett. *Bulletin of Miscellaneous Information (Royal Gardens, Kew)*, (1888), p. 160-63.

This is a short report on Fawcett's visit to the Cayman Islands in May 1888 to investigate diseased cocoa-nut palms. He describes the disease and its effects on the palms and gives a general commentary on the flora of the islands.

187 **Flora of the British West Indian islands.**
August Heinrich Rudolf Grisebach. London: Lovell Reeve, 1864. 789p.

Grisebach's work is a descriptive list of more than 3,400 species of flora found throughout the Caribbean. For each species, he provides a description, the scientific name and a location. However, there are no illustrations.

Birds

188 **Birds of the Cayman Islands.**
Patricia E. Bradley. Italy: Caerulea Press, 1995. rev. ed. 261p. 4 maps. bibliog.

Birds of the Cayman Islands was first published in 1985. In this revised edition, Bradley updates the status of all known birds and their habitats. She has also added new records to the 120 North American migrants and 45 breeding species listed in the first edition. There are summaries on climate; geography and geology; the origins of the avifauna; breeding and non-breeding species; and four local habitat zones and the kinds of plants characteristic of each zone. The individual species' accounts give physical descriptions, range, preferred Cayman habitat and habits. There are 77 full-colour plates. Appendix I contains a list of rarities, a bibliography of recommended field guides and a checklist of breeding birds, including the island on which each breeds. Appendix II addresses 'birding' in the Caymans. There is also a useful Phototips section.

189   **The avifauna of the Cayman Islands.**
Patricia E. Bradley. In: *The Cayman Islands: natural history and biogeography*. Edited by M. A. Brunt, J. E. Davies.   Dordrecht, Netherlands: Kluwer Academic Publishers, 1994, p. 377-406. (Monographiae Biologicae, vol. 71).
Bradley outlines the ornithological history of the islands from 1886 to 1991 and the derivation of the avifauna. She discusses the variety of species that are found and provides tables giving the species' distribution and status. There is also information on habitats and feeding habits.

190   **A field guide to birds of the West Indies.**
James Bond.   Boston, Massachusetts: Houghton Mifflin, 1993. 5th ed. 256p. (The Peterson Field Guide Series, 18).
This is a guide to the birds that inhabit the Greater and Lesser Antilles and the Bahama Islands. It is very complete and detailed in its coverage. Each species is presented by order, family and genus. There are two indexes, one of common names and one of local names, both of which are very useful. However, a geographical approach would have been appropriate as would the inclusion of maps.

191   **Boobies and frigates: strange bedfellows.**
Nancy Sefton.   *Sea Frontiers*, vol. 32, no. 4 (July/Aug. 1986), p. 290-95.
Both the red-footed booby and the frigate bird are found throughout the Caribbean. Sefton describes the booby's ability to retrieve food from the sea and the frigate bird's practice of attacking boobies in mid-air to take this food from them. Despite these hostilities, the booby and the frigate bird quite often nest together. This article is based on Sefton's observations of a rookery on Little Cayman where this co-habitation exists. She describes the birds' habitats and nesting habits.

192   **Ecology of the West Indian red-bellied woodpecker on Grand Cayman: distribution and foraging.**
Alexander Cruz, David W. Johnston.   *Wilson Bulletin*, vol. 96, no. 3 (Sept. 1984), p. 366-79.
The West Indian red-bellied woodpecker is widely distributed throughout the Caribbean region. The authors have identified it as a good species for the study of geographic variations in foraging behaviour; in differential sexual foraging related to regional variations in the quality and quantity of food; and in the intensity of its interactions with other woodpeckers. This study began in 1965 and continued intermittently until 1974. The 800 hours spent in the field covered all seasons. The authors provide data on distribution and habitat preference, food and foraging ecology, and differential feeding between the sexes. There are five tables of data accompanying the article.

193   **Ecology and species turnover of the birds of Little Cayman.**
       A. W. Diamond.   *Atoll Research Bulletin*, no. 241 (March 1980),
       p. 141-63.

Diamond's objectives are to determine what species are present on Little Cayman and the status of those species; to describe the ecology of each species particularly in relation to habitat and food; to draw attention to species which may be in need of special conservation methods; and to identify any habitat in need of special conservation methods because of its importance to birds. Diamond also discusses the derivation of the bird species (from the Greater Antilles, especially Cuba) and the distinctiveness of the various species (how many are endemic, how many are non-endemic). There are tables which list the species and their distribution, the endemic land birds of the Cayman Islands and their distribution, breeding records, and the habitats of breeding birds. An appendix gives a systematic list of the avifauna. The article is followed by a map and a chart on two unnumbered pages.

194   **The red-footed booby colony on Little Cayman: size, structure and significance.**
       A. W. Diamond.   *Atoll Research Bulletin*, no. 241 (March 1980),
       p. 165-69.

This colony is one of the largest and most accessible in the Caribbean. Diamond's objectives in the study, carried out in July and August 1975, were to estimate the size of the colony; to calculate the proportion of juveniles and adults; and to advise on the possible interaction between the colony and an oil terminal proposed for the island. Diamond estimated that, at the time, there were over 7100 boobies resident in the colony. The article is followed by a map and a chart on two unnumbered pages.

195   **Occurrence and feeding ecology of the Common Flicker on Grand Cayman.**
       Alexander Cruz, David W. Johnston.   *Condor*, vol. 81 (1979),
       p. 370-75.

This study began in 1965 and continued intermittently until 1973, covering all seasons. The objectives were to learn more about the distribution, habitat preferences, foods and foraging ecology of these birds and to compare the data with information on mainland flickers. The authors found that these birds were resident throughout Grand Cayman and they foraged primarily on arboreal ants and termites.

196   **Ecological analysis of the Cayman Island avifauna.**
       David W. Johnston.   *Bulletin of the Florida State Museum, Biological Sciences*, vol. 19, no. 5 (1975), p. 235-300.

Johnston's studies were carried out over a period of 8 years from ca. 1965-73. In this report, he describes seasonal occurrences and the relative abundance of birds, discusses the problems of inter-island distributional patterns and analyses the competition for environmental resources among resident terrestrial birds. Johnston focuses his attention on population densities, competitive interactions, food and feeding behaviours, reproductive cycles, predators and other population controls, and habitat distribution.

197   **Avifauna of the Cayman Islands.**
David W. Johnston, Charles H. Blake, Donald W. Buden.   *Quarterly Journal of the Florida Academy of Sciences*, vol. 34, no. 2 (June 1971), p. 141-56.

The authors begin with a description of the landforms and geology of the islands together with information about vegetation and topography. The bulk of the article is an annotated list of 151 species found in the Cayman Islands. For each species, the authors give the scientific and common names and an indication of distribution. They also list early collectors and the bibliographic references to their research.

198   **The thrushes of Grand Cayman Island, B.W.I.**
David W. Johnston.   *Condor*, vol. 71 (1969), p. 120-28.

Johnston's paper combines biological facts from the literature and information gathered from an examination of all 21 extant specimens of Mimocichla ravida, together with material from his own field studies on Grand Cayman between May 1965 and April 1967. He concludes that, since no thrushes had been seen on the island since 1938, the species is extinct.

199   **A collection of birds from the Cayman Islands.**
Outram Bangs.   *Bulletin of the Museum of Comparative Zoology*, vol. 60, no. 7 (1916), p. 303-20.

This is an annotated list of the species collected by W. W. Brown, Jr. in 1911. There are 41 species and subspecies listed and described. The descriptions range from one sentence to one page in length. Bangs also includes a commentary on Lowe's 1911 *Ibis* list of birds (q.v.) and his thoughts on the origins of some of the species.

200   **Notes on some of the birds of Grand Cayman, West Indies.**
T. M. Savage English.   *Ibis*, 10th series, vol. 4 (1916), p. 17-35.

Savage English adds twelve species to Lowe's 1911 list of 75 species (q.v.). He describes the twelve new species as well as eleven others.

201   **On the birds of the Cayman Islands, West Indies.**
Percy R. Lowe.   *Ibis*, 9th series, vol. 5 (1911), p. 137-61.

Following introductory remarks on geology, flora and early collecting expeditions, Lowe lists 75 species and sub-species, and indicates the habitat of each.

202   **A list of birds collected by Mr. C. J. Maynard in the islands of Little Cayman and Cayman Brack, West Indies.**
Charles B. Cory.   *Auk*, vol. 6 (1889), p. 30-32.

Cory lists 15 species found on Little Cayman and 29 species found on Cayman Brac. Interestingly, only five resident species of Grand Cayman are found on either Little Cayman or Cayman Brac.

203 **Descriptions of thirteen new species of birds from the Island of Grand Cayman, West Indies.**
Charles B. Cory.   *Auk*, vol. 3 (1886), p. 497-501.
Cory provides a detailed description for each of the thirteen species.

204 **A list of birds collected in the Island of Grand Cayman, West Indies, by W. B. Richardson, during the summer of 1886.**
Charles B. Cory.   *Auk*, vol. 3 (1886), p. 501-02.
This is a list of 40 species, thirteen of which Cory believes to be new. There are no details or descriptions, simply a list of names.

Insects

205 **Insects of the Cayman Islands.**
R. R. Askew. In: *The Cayman Islands: natural history and biogeography.*   Edited by M. A. Brunt, J. E. Davies.   Dordrecht, Netherlands: Kluwer Academic Publishers, 1994, p. 333-56.
(Monographiae Biologicae, vol. 71).
Askew's article begins with a brief history of entomology and entomological studies in the islands. Insects outnumber all other species on the islands 6 to 1. There is a table which lists butterfly species found in the islands during field trips conducted in 1938, 1975 and 1985 along with notes on some of the species. There are also comments on some of the more interesting insect species from the Caymans.

206 **Mosquitoes of the Cayman Islands.**
J. E. Davies. In: *The Cayman Islands: natural history and biogeography.*   Edited by M. A. Brunt, J. E. Davies.   Dordrecht, Netherlands: Kluwer Academic Publishers, 1994, p. 357-76.
(Monographiae Biologicae, vol. 71).
Davies outlines both the early records of mosquitoes from 1834 onwards and the mosquito collections gathered since 1965. There are descriptions of 35 species and observations on mosquitoes and disease. Finally, a history of mosquito control from 1910 onwards highlights the work of the Mosquito Research and Control Unit.

207 **The butterfly (Lepidoptera, Rhopalocera) fauna of the Cayman Islands.**
R. R. Askew.   *Atoll Research Bulletin*, no. 241 (March 1980), p. 121-38.
Askew provides a comparison of the species collected during a trip in 1975 with the species found on the Oxford University Expedition of 1938. Forty Caymanian species are described briefly and there is a discussion of daily flight activity and distribution. Askew concludes that the butterfly fauna are unremarkable for content or number of

species but that general abundance is a feature. Also, there are no endemic full species but there are four subspecies known only from Little Cayman. The article is followed by five charts and graphs on five unnumbered pages.

208 Hawkmoths (Lep., Sphingidae) of Little Cayman.
R. R. Askew. *Atoll Research Bulletin*, no. 241 (March 1980), p. 139.

Askew lists five species recorded by K. Jordan from the 1938 Oxford University Expedition and six species newly found. There are no descriptions given.

209 The insect fauna of Little Cayman.
R. R. Askew. *Atoll Research Bulletin*, no. 241 (March 1980), p. 97-114.

This paper describes the general characteristics of the insect fauna together with a discussion of the various trapping and collecting methods which were used. Throughout the collecting period, Askew found 613 species from 17 orders and has concluded that Little Cayman shares much of its insect fauna with Jamaica and Cuba. The article is followed by one chart on one unnumbered page.

210 The Odonata of the Cayman Islands, British West Indies.
R. R. Askew. *Atoll Research Bulletin*, no. 241 (March 1980), p. 115-19.

Askew adds five species to the known species of dragonflies and gives brief descriptions of the thirteen species sighted during the collection period. He found that there are no known endemic forms of dragonfly on Little Cayman.

211 Some field methods used in Grand Cayman for trapping adult ceratopogonids (Diptera).
J. E. Davies, Marco Enrico Clifton Giglioli. *Mosquito News*, vol. 39, no. 1 (March 1979), p. 149-53.

The authors describe three methods of trapping mosquitoes: a modified light trap, a light trap without suction and a goat baited trap. A table of figures lists the average catch per night per trap, the maximum catch per night per trap and the number of nights on which traps were set.

212 The breeding sites and seasonal occurrence of *Culicoides furens* in Grand Cayman with notes on breeding sites of the *Culicoides insignis* (Diptera: Ceratopogonidae).
J. E. Davies, Marco Enrico Clifton Giglioli. *Mosquito News*, vol. 37, no. 3 (Sept. 1977), p. 414-23.

The authors learn that *C. furens*, the dominant species in the Caymans, favours bare mud and non-tidal areas as a breeding site rather than mud with pneumatophores and tidal areas. *C. insignis* favours fresh water reed swamps.

213   **Water levels and the emergence of *Culicoides furens* (Diptera: Ceratopogonidae) from mangrove swamps in Grand Cayman.**
J. E. Davies, Marco Enrico Clifton Giglioli. *Mosquito News*, vol. 37, no. 3 (Sept. 1977), p. 426-35.

Davies and Giglioli studied the effects of water levels on *C. furens* emergence in a non-tidal mangrove swamp. They found that slowly rising water levels stimulate pupation and emergence and could lead to increases in adult abundance; rapidly rising water levels also stimulate pupation and emergence but do not lead to adult abundance because of pupation mortality; most flooded larvae do not seek new water lines but continue their larval life until water levels fall and re-expose swamp mud; some emergence can take place in flooded conditions; and the exposure of swamp mud by falling water levels leads to bursts of emergence. These studies were conducted daily between December 1970 and June 1972.

214   **A field guide to the butterflies of the West Indies.**
Norman D. Riley.   London: Collins, 1975. 224p. map. bibliog.

This guide allows for the identification of butterflies with a minimum of difficulty. Riley provides an introduction to butterfly morphology and classification, along with information on the life cycle of the butterfly and collecting methodologies. In the main body of the book, he describes 293 species. Each entry includes the scientific and common names, a description and an indication of distribution. A glossary, a checklist and a distribution table are also included. Of the species described, thirty-six are found in the Cayman Islands.

215   **Insecticide studies at the Mosquito Research and Control Unit, Grand Cayman, B.W.I.**
J. A. Armstrong.   *Mosquito News*, vol. 31, no. 1 (March 1971), p. 1-11.

Armstrong discusses a variety of commercial insecticides and their effectiveness against mosquitoes. He provides details of the tests which were conducted on Grand Cayman, along with seven tables of data.

216   **The effectiveness of Flit MLO against *Aedes taeniorhynchus* larvae on Grand Cayman, British West Indies.**
J. A. Armstrong.   *Mosquito News*, vol. 29, no. 3 (Sept. 1969), p. 489-90.

A series of trials were carried out in June and July 1968 to determine the minimum dosage of Flit MLO required to provide effective mosquito control and to ascertain the effect of weathering, in particular sunlight and light rain showers, following application of the insecticide. Details of the study are given and results show that Flit MLO is an effective means of mosquito control. An accompanying table provides data on the mortality of mosquito larvae.

217 **Remarks on the relationships of the butterflies (excluding skippers) of the Cayman Islands.**
Harry K. Clench. *Occasional Papers on Mollusks. Museum of Comparative Zoology*, vol. 2, no. 31 (Sept. 25, 1964), p. 381-82.
In this short article, Clench indicates that although there is no evidence of a particular relationship between Cayman fauna and that of Jamaica, there is a distinct connection between the butterflies of the Cayman Islands and those of Cuba. He also points out that of the 32 known species of Cayman Island butterflies, only two are endemic to the islands.

218 **The Staphylinid beetles of the Cayman Islands.**
Richard E. Blackwelder. *Proceedings of the United States National Museum*, vol. 97, no. 3213 (1947), p. 117-23.
Blackwelder describes twenty species of beetles, eighteen of which were gathered by the 1938 Oxford University Expedition. Each entry includes the scientific name, an indication of where the specimen was found and a brief note where necessary. Only one species, *Bledius mandibularis* Erichson, is described in detail.

219 **A collection of Lepidoptera (Rhopalocera) from the Cayman Islands.**
G. D. Hale Carpenter, C. Bernard Lewis. *Annals of the Carnegie Museum*, vol. 29, article 13 (1943), p. 371-96.
This collection of butterflies was gathered in 1938 by the Oxford University Expedition. The authors list and describe 41 species with entries that range from one sentence to more than a page.

220 **Results of the Oxford University Cayman Islands Biological Expedition, 1938: Descriptions of nine new species of Cerambycidae (Col.).**
W. S. Fisher. *The Entomologist's Monthly Magazine*, vol. 77, no. 924 (May 1941), p. 108-15.
Fisher provides very full and detailed descriptions of these nine new beetle species.

221 **Cicadas collected in the Cayman Islands by the Oxford University Biological Expedition of 1938.**
William T. Davis. *Journal of the New York Entomological Society*, vol. 47, no. 3 (Sept. 1939), 207-13.
Members of the expedition collected 92 specimens which Davis has examined. He describes three species in detail: *Diceroprocta cleavesi*, *Diceroprocta caymanensis* and *Diceroprocta ovata*.

222 **Report on an agricultural survey in the Cayman Islands.**
W. H. Edwards.   Kingston, Jamaica: Government Printing Office,
1937. 40p. (Department of Science and Agriculture, Bulletin, new
series, no. 13).

Edwards' primary object was to study insect fauna in relation to crops. He was also
responsible for investigating any other agricultural problems which came to his
attention while visiting the islands. He outlines the history and geography of the
islands as they relate to introduced insect pests and plant diseases, agriculture in
general, the mosquito problem, and insecticides and fungicides. During his stay in the
Caymans, Edwards found that insect pests and diseases were attacking the most
important economic plants: coconuts, bananas, citrus fruits, yams, sweet potatoes and
sugar cane.

Vertebrates and invertebrates

223 **Late Quaternary fossil vertebrates from the Cayman Islands.**
G. S. Morgan. In: *The Cayman Islands: natural history and
biogeography.*   Edited by M. A. Brunt, J. E. Davies.   Dordrecht,
Netherlands: Kluwer Academic Publishers, 1994, p. 465-508.
(Monographiae Biologicae, vol. 71).

This review is based on fossils excavated in the Cayman Islands between 1964 and
1987. Morgan describes two species of Amphibia, twelve species of Reptilia, thirty-
four species of Aves and twelve species of Mammalia. In an appendix there are
descriptions of the fossil sites: ten from Grand Cayman, two from Little Cayman and
eight from Cayman Brac.

224 **Terrestrial invertebrates (other than insects) of the Cayman
Islands.**
M. V. Hounsome. In: *The Cayman Islands: natural history and
biogeography.* Edited by M. A. Brunt, J. E. Davies.   Dordrecht,
Netherlands: Kluwer Academic Publishers, 1994, p. 307-31.
(Monographiae Biologicae, vol. 71).

Hounsome describes and discusses 143 species of invertebrates, including worms,
wood lice, crabs, millipedes, centipedes, scorpions and spiders, ticks and mites, and
snails and slugs.

Mammals

225　**Mammals of the Cayman Islands.**
　　G. S. Morgan. In: *The Cayman Islands: natural history and*
　　biogeography. Edited by M. A. Brunt, J. E. Davies.　Dordrecht,
　　Netherlands: Kluwer Academic Publishers, 1994, p. 435-63.
　　(Monographiae Biologicae, vol. 71).

This summary of mammalian fauna is based on fieldwork conducted between 1976
and 1986. Eight species of bats are the only extant native mammals on the islands,
while three species of cetaceans (whales and dolphins) have been recorded in the
surrounding sea. Four species of rodents have been introduced to the islands. All the
species are described in detail.

Marine life

226　**Common sponges of the Cayman Islands.**
　　Joe Ghiold. In: *The Cayman Islands: natural history and*
　　biogeography. Edited by M. A. Brunt, J. E. Davies.　Dordrecht,
　　Netherlands: Kluwer Academic Publishers, 1994, p. 131-38.
　　(Monographiae Biologicae, vol. 71).

There are no published scientific reports of sponges in the Cayman Islands, only
incidental mentions. Thus, Ghiold's article on sponge morphology and habitats, and
sponge communities is an important contribution to the discipline.

227　**Echinoids of Grand Cayman.**
　　Joe Ghiold, G. A. Rountree. In: *The Cayman Islands: natural history*
　　and biogeography.　Edited by M. A. Brunt, J. E. Davies.　Dordrecht,
　　Netherlands: Kluwer Academic Publishers, 1994, p. 191-98.
　　(Monographiae Biologicae, vol. 71).

The authors discuss and list a variety of echinoids, or sea urchins, and describe four
particular species in detail: Lytechinus variegatus, Clypeaster rosaceus, Meoma
ventricosa and Diadema antiiarum.

228　**Fishes of the Cayman Islands.**
　　G. H. Burgess, Stephen H. Smith, E. D. Lane. In: *The Cayman Islands:*
　　natural history and biogeography.　Edited by M. A. Brunt,
　　J. E. Davies.　Dordrecht, Netherlands: Kluwer Academic Publishers,
　　1994, p. 199-228. (Monographiae Biologicae, vol. 71).

The authors provide descriptions of collections of ichthyofauna from the 1960s to the
1980s as well as descriptions of the various Cayman Islands marine habitats. There is
an annotated list of 381 species. The article also contains sections on inshore and

offshore sport fishing and commercial fisheries. There are two tables giving game fish records to June 1992 and captured billfish records from 1983 to 1991.

229 **Marine algae of the Cayman Islands: a preliminary account.**
I. Tittley. In: *The Cayman Islands: natural history and biogeography.*
Edited by M. A. Brunt, J. E. Davies. Dordrecht, Netherlands: Kluwer
Academic Publishers, 1994, p. 125-30. (Monographiae Biologicae,
vol. 71).

Tittley reports that the marine algal (seaweed) flora of the Cayman Islands are poorly
described compared to that of the rest of the Caribbean Sea. Tittley references some
studies and provides a checklist of 149 species of algae found in the Cayman Islands.

230 **Reefs and lagoons of Cayman Brac and Little Cayman.**
Alan Logan. In: *The Cayman Islands: natural history and
biogeography.* Edited by M. A. Brunt, J. E. Davies. Dordrecht,
Netherlands: Kluwer Academic Publishers, 1994, p. 105-24.
(Monographiae Biologicae, vol. 71).

Logan reports that the study of the reefs and lagoons of Cayman Brac and Little
Cayman has not been as complete as the studies conducted on Grand Cayman. This
article, however, is the first step towards a more detailed scientific investigation of the
submarine topography, lagoons and coral reefs of the Lesser Caymans.

231 **Reefs and lagoons of Grand Cayman.**
Harry Heil Roberts. In: *The Cayman Islands: natural history and
biogeography.* Edited by M. A. Brunt, J. E. Davies. Dordrecht,
Netherlands: Kluwer Academic Publishers, 1994, p. 75-104.
(Monographiae Biologicae, vol. 71).

Roberts discusses such topics as submarine topography, shelf and slope reefs, fringing
reefs, lagoons, and sediment transportation routes and sinks.

232 **Bleaching and recovery of deep-water, reef-dwelling invertebrates
in the Cayman Islands, B.W.I.**
Joe Ghiold, Stephen H. Smith. *Caribbean Journal of Science,*
vol. 26, no. 1-2 (June 1990), p. 52-61.

Coral bleaching occurs when zooanthellae are expelled from the host tissue leaving
the coral pale or white. This bleaching can interfere with the animal's energy
requirements. This paper documents the recovery or death of bleached corals,
describes the various species and reef zones affected by bleaching and examines the
speculation that bleaching in the Caribbean can be attributed to high water
temperatures or increased light intensity. The authors conclude that the duration and
severity of bleaching in the Caymans varies with species and depth of habitation.
There are four tables of data, one map and six black-and-white photographs.

233 **Ballet with stingrays.**
David Doubilet. *National Geographic*, vol. 175, no. 1 (Jan. 1989),
p. 84-95.

In this photographic essay, Doubilet shows the close relationship which has been
formed between humans and stingrays in North Sound off Grand Cayman. The
captions to the photographs provide some information about stingray feeding habits
and defence mechanisms.

234 **Looking for exotic marine life? Don't leave the dock.**
Franklin Jay Viola. *Sea Frontiers*, vol. 35, no. 6 (Nov./Dec. 1989),
p. 336-41.

Viola gives vivid descriptions and provides colour photographs of the wide variety of
exotic fishes and invertebrates, including sea squirts, shrimp, crabs, jellyfish and
starfish, which can be found in less than 3 metres of water almost anywhere along the
shores of the Cayman Islands.

235 **Marine plants of the Caribbean: a field guide from Florida to
Brazil.**
Diane Scullion Littler, Mark M. Littler, Katina E. Bucher, James N.
Norris. Washington, DC: Smithsonian Institution Press, 1989. 263p.
map. bibliog.

This work describes 204 species of algae and five species of seagrasses which
represent the common species most likely to be encountered in the waters of the
Caribbean. Each entry provides a brief description giving size, shape, colour, depth
and habitat along with a colour photograph. Technical terms are kept to a minimum
but a glossary has been appended. This guide is very useful for quick identification.

236 **Down the Cayman Wall.**
Eugenie Clark. *National Geographic*, vol. 174, no. 5 (Nov. 1988),
p. 712-31.

The Cayman Wall is a submarine escarpment that is part of Grand Cayman Island. It is
made up of four zones of marine life: the reef zone, an area of fishes and corals that
extends to a depth of two hundred feet; the wall zone, two hundred to six hundred feet,
that is home to sponges; the haystacks, six hundred to one thousand feet, where
portions of the wall which may have eroded and fallen down have created distinctive
formations – here are found sharks and starfish; and the deep, an area deeper than one
thousand feet, lacking in sunlight but abundant in strange species. Clark's article,
based on a year's research during the 1980s and more than one hundred dives,
contains marvellous colour photographs and a colour diagram detailing the Wall and
its four zones of life.

237 **Cayman seascapes: Paul Humann's portfolio of marine life.**
Paul Humann. Grand Cayman; Hollywood, Florida: Underwater
Specialists, 1986. 96p.

Humann has produced a book of spectacular colour photography accompanied by
some complementary text.

238 **A field guide to coral reefs: Caribbean and Florida.**
Eugene H. Kaplan. Boston, Massachusetts: Houghton Mifflin, 1982.
289p. map. bibliog. (The Peterson Field Guide Series, 27).

This book was sponsored by the National Audubon Society, the National Wildlife
Federation and the Roger Tory Peterson Institute. Following a very good introductory
chapter, Kaplan provides an overview of coral reefs, their development and their
ecology. The bulk of the work is devoted to the animals of the lagoon and the reef.
Technical terms are kept to a minimum as the book is intended for laypeople, though a
glossary is provided. The book is illustrated with 37 black-and-white and coloured
plates.

239 **Handguide to the coral reef fishes of the Caribbean and adjacent
tropical waters including Florida, Bermuda and the Bahamas.**
F. Joseph Stokes. New York: Lippincott & Crowell, 1980. 160p.

The emphasis in this guide is on the illustrations, which are paintings of colour
photographs, while the descriptions in the text often consist of only one sentence or
several short phrases. The 460 species described are the ones most likely to be seen by
the snorkeller and diver. This book, which includes a glossary, is useful for both
professionals and amateurs.

240 **The littoral fishes of Little Cayman (West Indies).**
G. W. Potts. *Atoll Research Bulletin*, no. 241 (March 1980), p. 43-52.

Potts provides a brief survey of the littoral marine fishes of Little Cayman, with notes
on their habitat preferences, and discusses the classification of littoral fish fauna. He
concludes that the fauna elements found in this area are typical of the rest of the
Caribbean. This supports the theory that the Caribbean is an integrated zoogeographic
unit. There are two tables, one of which lists the fifteen species discussed and
indicates their habitat preferences.

241 **Seashore life of Florida and the Caribbean: a guide to the common
marine invertebrates and plants of the Atlantic from Bermuda and
the Bahamas to the West Indies and the Gulf of Mexico.**
Gilbert L. Voss. Miami, Florida: Banyan, 1980. rev. ed. 199p. map.
bibliog.

The species which Voss includes in this guide represent only a small part of the total
fauna: those that one might reasonably expect to find down to a depth of fifty feet.
Nevertheless, this book includes a great many species from thirteen invertebrate phyla
(sponges, jellyfish, corals, sea anemones, sea fans, flatworms, ribbon worms, sea
slugs, squids, crustaceans, sea stars, sea urchins and sea cucumbers) and four plant
phyla (algae and sea grasses). Each entry is written in simple language. There are also
400 drawings and 19 very good colour photographs.

242 **Fishes of the Caribbean reefs, the Bahamas and Bermuda.**
Ian F. Took. London: Macmillan, 1979. 92p. map.

Took's work is an introduction to some of the more common and spectacular fish to be
found around the Caribbean and tropical west Atlantic reefs. For each of the eighty-
five species covered, he provides a description, including length; common and
scientific names; a discussion of general habits and particular characteristics; and an

indication of where the fish might be found. There are also sections on practical fish watching, underwater photography and conservation of the coral reef. The work is illustrated with seventy-two colour plates of fish and seven of coral.

243 **Caribbean reef invertebrates and plants: a field guide to the invertebrates and plants occurring on coral reefs of the Caribbean, the Bahamas and Florida.**
Patrick Lynn Colin.   Hong Kong: T. F. H. Publications, 1978. 512p. map. bibliog.

This book is designed to serve as an identification guide for the professional marine scientist and the amateur snorkeller or scuba diver. Colin provides good introductory chapters on the natural history of Caribbean reefs and their organisms. The entries are arranged by phylum, with animals preceding plants. Within each phylum, the individual species are considered by order and family. The descriptions given for each entry are very good, while the black-and-white and colour photographs are adequate. Sponges, sea fans and sea anemones, corals, marine worms, crustaceans, molluscs, starfish, sea urchins and sea cucumbers, and marine plants and algae are all included.

244 **Cayman Islands natural resources study: results of the investigations into the coral reefs and marine parks.**
J. E. G. Raymont, A. P. M. Lockwood, Laurence E. Hull, Geoffrey W. J. Swain.   London: Ministry of Overseas Development, 1976. 26p. map. bibliog. (Cayman Islands Natural Resources Study, part IV B).

The fifth volume of the *Cayman Islands natural resources study* (q.v.) describes the marine flora and fauna found on the coral reefs of Grand Cayman Island. The authors recommend eight sites for marine parks and outline some suggestions for control and development.

245 **Cayman Islands natural resources study: results of the investigations into the marine biology.**
J. E. G. Raymont, A. P. M. Lockwood, Laurence E. Hull, Geoffrey W. J. Swain.   London: Ministry of Overseas Development, 1976. 130p. 8 maps. (Cayman Islands Natural Resources Study, part IV A).

In the fourth volume of the *Cayman Islands natural resources study* (q.v.), the authors discuss marine flora and fauna and provide information on water temperature, sea grass and mangrove areas, and artificial reefs. A 20-page appendix lists all species of marine flora and fauna found in the islands.

246 **Seashells of the West Indies: a guide to marine molluscs of the Caribbean.**
Michael Humfrey.   New York: Taplinger, 1975. 351p. map. bibliog. (Taplinger World Wide Field Guides).

This guide was written primarily for somebody seriously beginning to collect seashells for the first time but is also useful for the professional or experienced amateur. It is designed to achieve four purposes: to provide a general illustrated guide to West Indian marine shells; to examine the habitat of each of the 497 shells described and illustrated; to provide a census of all known Jamaican marine molluscs; and to examine in detail the most efficient methods of collecting, cleaning and storing shells. Each entry lists the scientific and popular names, and the range, description and occurrence of the species. There is also a good introductory section in which Humfrey discusses mollusc classification and structure, environment, feeding and breeding habits, identification and distribution.

247 **In the coral reefs of the Caribbean, Bahamas, Florida, Bermuda.**
Hans W. Hannau.   Garden City, New York: Doubleday, 1974. 135p.
This general introduction to coral reefs is accompanied by ninety-four colour plates. Each chapter is by a different contributor which does lead to a patchy quality, and to over-simplified material being combined with highly technical information. There are useful chapters on corals, molluscs, fish and reef ecology but this picture-book for the 'armchair' explorer would be improved by maps and an index.

248 **Observations on the vegetative culture of Plexaura homomalla in the Cayman Islands.**
Robert E. Schroeder. In: *Prostaglandins from Plexaura homomalla: ecology, utilization and conservation of a major medical marine resource, a symposium.*   Edited by Frederick M. Bayer, Alfred J. Weinheimer.   Coral Gables, Florida: University of Miami Press, 1974, p. 111-14. (Studies in Tropical Oceanography, 12).
Experiments were conducted to determine the feasibility of the commercial culture of *Plexaura homomalla* as a source of prostaglandins. Artificial substrates and methods of attachment were devised, and the viability and rate of growth of both large and small cuttings were compared. Schroeder provides no definite conclusions.

249 **Studies on experimental harvesting and regrowth of *Plexaura homomalla* in Grand Cayman waters.**
J. W. Hinman, S. R. Anderson, Marlin Simon. In: *Prostaglandins from Plexaura homomalla: ecology, utilization and conservation of a major medical marine resource, a symposium.*   Edited by Frederick M. Bayer, Alfred J. Weinheimer.   Coral Gables, Florida: University of Miami Press, 1974, p. 39-57. (Studies in Tropical Oceanography, 12).
Studies were undertaken to determine the quality of *Plexaura homomalla* present in the area, the ecologically acceptable methods of harvesting the product, the feasibility of artificial mariculture, the impact of harvesting on the ecology of the reefs, and the growth rates and reproduction of the product. The authors conclude that *Plexaura homomalla* can be harvested by methods which permit regrowth and do not inflict any discernible damage to the ecosystem.

250 **Beneath the seas of the West Indies: Caribbean, Bahamas, Florida, Bermuda.**
Hans W. Hannau, Bernd H. Mock.   New York: Hastings House, 1973. 104p.
The authors discuss reefs, reef ecology and marine archaeology in the West Indies. The book includes fifty-four large colour plates and 120 small colour plates, as well as a picture portfolio for the identification of exotic tropical fish which inhabit reef areas.

251 **Caribbean reef fishes.**
John E. Randall.   Jersey City, New Jersey: T.F.H. Publications, 1968.
318p.

Randall's primary purpose is to identify the 300 most common fishes that might be observed while snorkelling or diving on the reefs of the Caribbean Sea. The species examined are arranged in approximate phylogenetic sequence beginning with cartilaginous fishes, i.e. sharks and rays. For each fish discussed, Randall gives an illustration, the common and scientific names, the length and description, and an indication of location. Most illustrations are black and white; colour plates are limited. There is a glossary of ichthyological terms.

252 **Caribbean seashells: a guide to the marine mollusks of Puerto Rico and other West Indian Islands, Bermuda and the lower Florida Keys.**
Germaine Le Clerc Warmke, Robert Tucker Abbott.   Norberth,
Pennsylvania: Livingston, 1961. 348p. 21 maps. bibliog.

Warmke and Abbott provide information on periwinkles, conches and other snails (Class Gastropoda), scallops, oysters and other clams (Class Pelecypoda), and squids, chitons and tusk shells (Classes Cephalopoda, Amphineura and Scaphopoda). There are thirty-four black-and-white drawings in the text along with four colour and forty black-and-white plates. Entries include a description and distribution range, as well as the scientific and common names of each specimen.

Crustaceans

253 *Tisbe caymanensis*, **a new species of Copepod from Grand Cayman, B.W.I.**
Harry C. Yeatman.   *Journal of the Tennessee Academy of Science*,
vol. 59, no. 3 (July 1984), p. 46-48.

Yeatman gives a detailed description of a new species of harpacticoid copepod using male and female specimens collected from a drainage ditch on Grand Cayman.

Molluscs

254 Marine molluscs of the Cayman Islands.

D. F. Hess, Robert Tucker Abbott, J. Hamann, K. Meyer, S. Millen, T. Gosliner, Nancy Sefton, Roger T. Hanlon. In: *The Cayman Islands: natural history and biogeography.* Edited by M. A. Brunt, J. E. Davies. Dordrecht, Netherlands: Kluwer Academic Publishers, 1994, p. 139-89. (Monographiae Biologicae, vol. 71).

An introduction outlines studies undertaken between 1901 and 1992 and is followed by an annotated checklist containing 423 species from Gastropoda: Prosobranchia, Gastropoda: Opisthobranchia, Gastropoda: Pulmonata, Polyplacophora, Scaphapoda, Bivalvia and Cephalopoda. An appendix lists Pleistocene molluscs.

255 *Cerion nanus* (Maynard) (Mollusca: Ceriondae) on Little Cayman.

M. V. Hounsome, R. R. Askew. *Atoll Research Bulletin*, no. 241 (March 1980), p. 91-95.

This species was first collected and described by Charles Johnson Maynard in 1888-89. It has a restricted distribution on Little Cayman. The authors discuss the localities in which it is found and the numbers which are prevalent. The article is followed by three unnumbered pages containing three black-and-white plates.

256 A field guide to shells: Atlantic and Gulf Coasts and the West Indies.

Percy A. Morris. Edited by William J. Clench. Boston, Massachusetts: Houghton Mifflin, 1975. 3rd ed. 330p. bibliog. (The Peterson Field Guide Series, 3).

Like many of the Peterson Field Guides, this one was sponsored by the National Audubon Society, the National Wildlife Federation and the Roger Tory Peterson Institute. Morris describes 1,035 species and subspecies of shells and all but two are illustrated. Each description includes the common and scientific names, the geographical range, the habitat, and a physical description. The shells described are divided into five classes: pelecypods, gastropods, amphineurans, scaphopods and cephalopods. The appendices contain a glossary, a list of the authors referred to in the descriptions, a bibliography and a list of east coast shell clubs.

257 Land and freshwater mollusca of the Cayman Islands, West Indies.

William J. Clench. *Occasional Papers on Mollusks. Museum of Comparative Zoology*, vol. 2, no. 31 (Sept. 25, 1964), p. 345-80.

Following a general introduction to the topology of the Cayman Islands, Clench outlines previous collections from the 1880s to the 1940s. According to his studies, 30 of the 48 recorded species are endemic to the islands. Seventeen of these show a relationship with the species of Jamaica, ten with Cuba, two with Central America and one with the Isle of Pines. Clench gives an annotated list of all 48 known species, with three species (Cerion pannosum, Cerion martinianum and Cerion nanus) being described in great detail. There is also a chart indicating the distribution of the species throughout the Cayman Islands.

258   The marine mollusks of Grand Cayman Island, British West
      Indies.
      Robert Tucker Abbott.   Philadelphia, Pennsylvania: Academy of
      Natural Sciences of Philadelphia, 1958. 138p. 11 maps. bibliog.
      (Monographs of the Academy of Natural Sciences of Philadelphia, 11).
This taxonomic and ecological study of shallow-water marine molluscs is based on
collections made at 160 localities on Grand Cayman. Abbott gives detailed
descriptions of 293 species of gastropoda, amphineura, scaphopoda, pelecypoda and
cephalopoda. There are also five black-and-white plates.

259   Mollusca of the University of Oxford Expedition to the Cayman
      Islands in 1938.
      A. E. Salisbury.   *Proceedings of the Malacological Society of London*,
      vol. 30 (May 1953), p. 39-54.
Salisbury lists and describes 61 species from the classes Cephalopoda,
Polyplacophora, Gastropoda and Lamellibranchia. For each entry there is a physical
description of the species and an indication of its distribution. Salisbury also supplies
a description of a supposed new Chiton.

260   Results of the Catherwood-Chaplin West Indies Expedition, 1948.
      Part IV: Land snails of North Cat Cay (Bahamas), Cayo Largo
      (Cuba), Grand Cayman, Saint Andrews and Old Providence.
      Charles B. Wurtz.   *Proceedings of the Academy of Natural Sciences
      of Philadelphia*, vol. 102 (1950), p. 95-110.
The researchers spent one day on Grand Cayman and collected 21 species at six
stations across the island. Wurtz has listed the species collected and describes five of
them. Five species were collected on North Cat Cay, eight on Cayo Largo, thirteen on
Saint Andrews and nine on Old Providence Island.

261   Land mollusks of Cayman Brac.
      Henry A. Pilsbry.   *Nautilus*, vol. 63, no. 2 (Oct. 1949), p. 37-48.
Pilsbry describes eleven species of land molluscs from Cayman Brac in detail. His
observations are based on specimens collected by C. Bernard Lewis in 1940.

262   Land mollusca of the Cayman Islands collected by the Oxford
      University Biological Expedition, 1938.
      Henry A. Pilsbry.   *Nautilus*, vol. 56, no. 1 (July 1942), p. 1-9.
Pilsbry describes six new species and three new subspecies of land molluscs. He also
lists twenty-two other species which were collected.

263   **Results of the Pinchot South Sea Expedition – I: Land mollusks of the Caribbean islands, Grand Cayman, Swan, Old Providence and St. Andrew.**
Henry A. Pilsbry. *Proceedings of the Academy of Natural Sciences of Philadelphia*, vol. 82 (1930), p. 221-61.
In the section on the land molluscs of Grand Cayman (p. 224-39), Pilsbry describes 24 of the 29 species which were collected in May 1929. He gives detailed descriptions of twelve new species. There is also a discussion of the origins of the Grand Cayman species and their relation to species found in Jamaica, Cuba and Puerto Rico.

264   **Results of the Pinchot South Sea Expedition – II: Land mollusks of the Canal Zone, the Republic of Panama, and the Cayman Islands.**
Henry A. Pilsbry. *Proceedings of the Academy of Natural Sciences of Philadelphia*, vol. 82 (1930), p. 339-54.
The specimens were collected in May 1929. Pilsbry describes 45 species in detail. In an appendix, he provides additional data on land molluscs of the Cayman Islands and describes six species, two of which are new.

Reptiles

265   **Amphibians and reptiles (exclusive of marine turtles) of the Cayman Islands.**
Michael E. Seidel, R. Franz. In: *The Cayman Islands: natural history and biogeography*. Edited by M. A. Brunt, J. E. Davies. Dordrecht, Netherlands: Kluwer Academic Publishers, 1994, p. 407-33.
(Monographiae Biologicae, vol. 71).
The authors describe in detail only three species of Amphibia: Eleutherodactylus planirostris planirostris (greenhouse frog), Osteopilus septentrionalis (Cuban treefrog) and Gastrophryne carolinensis (Eastern narrowmouth frog). They also describe 23 species of Reptilia in detail. They discuss the distributional relationships of Caymanian amphibians and reptiles; the effect of exotic amphibians and reptiles being introduced to the islands; and the impact of and need for conservation. Seidel and Franz conclude that the fauna has remained stable since the late Pleistocene but is now at a crossroads.

266   **Sea turtles of the Cayman Islands.**
F. E. Wood, J. R. Wood. In: *The Cayman Islands: natural history and biogeography*. Edited by M. A. Brunt, J. E. Davies. Dordrecht, Netherlands: Kluwer Academic Publishers, 1994, p. 229-36.
(Monographiae Biologicae, vol. 71).
The four species of sea turtle occurring in the Cayman Islands are discussed and described: Chelonia mydas (green sea turtle), Eretmochelys imbricata (hawksbill

turtle), Caretta caretta (loggerhead turtle) and Dermochelys coriacea (leatherback turtle). The authors also provide information on the natural history of the sea turtle and its habitats in the Cayman Islands, and the status of the turtling industry in the islands.

267 **Seafarers of the Caymans.**
Nancy Sefton. *Sea Frontiers*, vol. 35, no. 2 (March/April 1989), p. 106-13.
Sefton presents a concise history of turtling from 1503 to the present day.

268 **Observations on habitat utilization by the lizard *Anolis conspersus* on the island of Grand Cayman, West Indies.**
R. A. Avery. *Amphibia-Reptilia*, vol. 9, no. 4 (Nov. 1988), p. 417-20.
Avery observed this species, which is endemic to Grand Cayman, over a three week period from 11 February to 2 March 1987. He examined the lizard's distribution patterns and habitat in both forest/scrub habitat and open habitat. Avery also observed the lizard's positions and movements on and above ground.

269 **Salinity tolerance of estuarine and insular emydid turtles (*Pseudemys nelsoni* and *Trachemys decussata*).**
William A. Dunson, Michael E. Seidel. *Journal of Herpetology*, vol. 20, no. 2 (1986), p. 237-45.
These turtles inhabit brackish water in mainland areas in the extreme south of Florida and on Grand Cayman Island. Their natural habitats vary seasonally in salinity but remain on average quite dilute due to rainfall. This study was undertaken to determine salinity levels and the turtles' tolerance within those levels.

270 **Dragons of Cayman.**
David Blair. *Oceans*, vol. 16, no. 2 (March/April 1983), p. 31-33.
This article describes Blair's trip to Little Cayman in late 1982 to photograph the Cayman Island rock iguana (*Cyclura nubilia caymanensis*). These reptiles are found only in the Cayman Islands and can reach a length of almost five feet and a weight of up to twenty pounds. Although chiefly herbivorous, they may eat young rodents, insects and carrion. Blair provides information on breeding and feeding habits.

271 **The windward road: adventures of a naturalist on remote Caribbean shores.**
Archie Fairly Carr. Tallahassee, Florida: University Presses of Florida, 1979. 258p. 3 maps. (A Florida State University Book).
Carr's purpose in researching and writing this book was to collect and disseminate information on sea turtles. The book is much more than just a scientific treatise. Carr does provide the information he promises, but also gives the reader an excellent sense of the Caribbean lifestyle. The chapters entitled 'The Captains' (p. 206-36) and 'The Passing of the Fleet' (p. 237-52) give information about turtling and turtle fishermen in the Cayman Islands. There are seventeen black-and-white photographs and a glossary. This is a reprint of the 1956 edition (New York: Knopf) with a new preface.

272 **The green sea turtle of the Cayman Islands.**
James L. Considine. *Oceanus*, vol. 21, no. 3 (Summer 1978),
p. 50-55.
Considine discusses the history of turtle fishing and expresses concern about the
possible extinction of the green sea turtle (*Chelonia mydas mydas*), also called the
Atlantic Green Turtle. He also provides information on turtle farming which was
introduced to the Cayman Islands by Mariculture, Ltd. in 1968.

273 **So excellent a fishe: a natural history of sea turtles.**
Archie Fairly Carr. Garden City, New York: Natural History Press,
1967. 248p. 2 maps.
Carr presents a thorough study of all aspects of the natural history of the sea turtle,
and discusses the creature's importance to the development of the Cayman Islands.

274 **Terrapin from Grand Cayman.**
T. Barbour, Archie Fairly Carr, Jr. *Proceedings of the New England
Zoological Club*, vol. 18 (Aug. 7, 1941), p. 57-60.
The authors speculate on the origins of land or fresh-water turtles on the Cayman
Islands. They wonder how the species were introduced but cannot provide a clear
answer. After examining specimens of a new species given to the Museum of
Comparative Zoology by Major Chapman Grant, Barbour and Carr named the new
species *Pseudemys granti*. A detailed description of the new species is included.

275 **The herpetology of the Cayman Islands, with an appendix on the
Cayman Islands and marine turtle.**
Chapman Grant, C. Bernard Lewis. Kingston, Jamaica: Institute of
Jamaica, 1940. 65p. (Bulletin of the Institute of Jamaica. Science
Series, no. 2).
In *The herpetology of the Cayman Islands* (p. 1-56), Grant reviews the history of
Cayman herpetology and then provides a systematic account of the species with
information on two classes, Amphibia and Reptilia; three orders; two sub-orders;
and ten families. His detailed information includes species description, dimensions
and proportions, colour patterns, sexual dimorphism and relationships, habits and
distribution. In his appendix (p. 56-65), Lewis outlines the history of the turtle
industry through the use of extensive quotes from a variety of sources. Although this
overview is useful, Lewis does not provide the full bibliographic details for his
sources.

276 **Reptiles and batrachians from the Caymans and from the
Bahamas.**
Samuel Garman. *Bulletin of the Essex Institute*, vol. 20 (1888),
p. 101-13.
This paper is a sequel to Garman's 1887 paper (q.v.) concerning specimens from
Grand Cayman. Since there were no previous studies for Little Cayman or Cayman
Brac, Garman's work becomes the first in this area. All the species reported from
Little Cayman are of Cuban origin, while those reported from Cayman Brac are of
both Cuban and Jamaican origin. Garman describes seven species from Cayman Brac

and six species from Little Cayman. He also describes eight species from the Bahamas.

277 On the reptiles and batrachians of Grand Cayman.

Samuel Garman. *Proceedings of the American Philosophical Society*, vol. 24, no. 126 (1887), p. 273-77.

The collection upon which this paper is based contained 105 specimens, accounting for three species of lizard and one species each of snake, toad and treefrog. Garman describes six species in great detail: Anolis conspersus, Liocephalus varius, and Aristelliger praesignis (all lizards); Alsophis caymanus (snake); Bufo marinus (toad); and Hyla septentrionalis (treefrog).

Environment

278 **The boom years in Grand Cayman; environmental deterioration and conservation.**
Marco Enrico Clifton Giglioli. In: *The Cayman Islands: natural history and biogeography.* Edited by M. A. Brunt, J. E. Davies. Dordrecht, Netherlands: Kluwer Academic Publishers, 1994, p. 509-26. (Monographiae Biologicae, vol. 71).
Giglioli defines the economic boom years as 1965 to 1974. He discusses their impact on the island and provides information on the land, swamp and water areas, turbidity and reclamation techniques employed during this period. This article is based heavily on his contribution to the second volume of the *Cayman Islands natural resources study* (q.v.). J. E. Davies provides an update on development since 1975.

279 **Conservation in Grand Cayman: one island's chance to make it work.**
Dennis Anderson. *Oceans*, vol. 17, no. 5 (Sept./Oct. 1984), p. 38-45, 48-49.
Anderson outlines the conservation measures taken from the 1950s to the 1970s and highlights the work of Marco Giglioli, Nancy Sefton and Jack Andersen.

280 **Turtle trouble on Grand Cayman.**
Michael Bean. *Defenders*, vol. 58, no. 1-2 (Feb./March/April 1983), p. 14-19.
Bean outlines conservationists' concerns regarding turtle farming and outlines steps which have been taken to curtail or shut down operations.

281 **Geography and ecology of Little Cayman.**
Edited by D. R. Stoddart, Marco Enrico Clifton Giglioli.
Washington, DC: Smithsonian Institution, March 1980. 180p. 10 maps.
(Atoll Research Bulletin, 241).

This item contains sixteen articles which resulted from an expedition to Little Cayman in 1975. The purpose of the expedition was to define and characterize the major terrestrial and shallow marine habitats of the island and to describe the major features of the marine and terrestrial biota in order to provide background information for any future development. The expedition was sponsored by the Royal Society of London and the Cayman Islands Government. The articles are listed separately in this bibliography under the appropriate categories.

282 **Little Cayman: ecology and significance.**
D. R. Stoddart. *Atoll Research Bulletin*, no. 241 (March 1980),
p. 171-80.

Stoddart reviews the conclusions of the contributors to *Geography and ecology of Little Cayman* (q.v.) and considers some of the gaps in the knowledge of the ecology of Little Cayman. In particular, he discusses the extinct species, the species at risk, the habitats at risk and the marine habitats which should become reserves. The article is followed by a map on an unnumbered page.

283 **Scientific study of Little Cayman.**
D. R. Stoddart. *Atoll Research Bulletin*, no. 241 (March 1980),
p. 1-10.

In this introductory article to *Geography and ecology of Little Cayman* (q.v.), Stoddart outlines the various scientific studies which have been undertaken beginning with the work of Charles Johnson Maynard in 1888. There is also general information about rainfall, winds and currents.

284 **Still no ban on green turtle imports.**
Jeremy Cherfas. *New Scientist*, vol. 85, no. 1200 (March 27, 1980),
p. 988.

This is a follow-up to Cherfas' 1979 article (q.v.). He re-iterates conservationists' concerns and reviews the legal actions which have been taken.

285 **No end to trade in turtles.**
Jeremy Cherfas. *New Scientist*, vol. 84, no. 1185 (Dec. 13, 1979),
p. 852.

Cherfas explains that conservationists are concerned about the turtle trade from the Cayman Islands. However, the Cayman Turtle Farm meets the criteria as outlined in the Convention of International Trade in Endangered Species (CITES) and the British government will, therefore, not deter imports from the farm.

286 **Cayman Islands natural resources study.**
London: Ministry of Overseas Development, 1976. 6 vols.

This massive study was undertaken to determine the nature and extent of the natural marine resources of the Cayman Islands, their current and potential importance to the islands, and the current and foreseeable damage to which those resources might be subjected. Researchers were also asked to recommend legislation and other measures for the utilization and preservation of those resources. The individual volumes are listed separately under appropriate headings elsewhere in this bibliography.

287   **Cayman Islands natural resources study: final report and recommendations.**
J. H. Wickstead.   London: Ministry of Overseas Development, 1976.
vol. 1. 2 maps. (Cayman Islands Natural Resources Study, part I).

The first volume of the *Cayman Islands natural resources study* (q.v.) contains 12 individual reports on a variety of subjects including tourism, beach litter and rubbish, oil pollution, dredging and canal development, mangroves, coral reefs and marine parks and fisheries. There are also two sections of recommendations. The first section lists recommendations on dredging for marine sand in North Sound and the second gives recommendations for the rest of Grand Cayman and the lesser Cayman Islands.

288   **Cayman Islands natural resources study: the boom years, environmental deterioration, planning and administration.**
Marco Enrico Clifton Giglioli.   London: Ministry of Overseas Development, 1976. 42p. 6 maps. bibliog. (Cayman Islands Natural Resources Study, part II).

In the second volume of the *Cayman Islands natural resources study* (q.v.), Giglioli discusses the need for and the background to the study. He also provides information on the land, swamp and water areas, turbidity and reclamation techniques.

Prehistory and Archaeology

289 **The Caymanian catboat.**
   Roger C. Smith. *World Archaeology*, vol. 16, no. 3 (Feb. 1985),
   p. 329-36.

Prior to 1900, turtling canoes were used to hunt turtles around the Cayman Islands. In 1904 a prototype of the Caymanian catboat was built by Daniel Jervis, a turtling captain from Cayman Brac. One surviving example was found in the 1980s. Smith provides a photograph and drawings of the catboat which is similar in design to the New England whaleboat and the Newfoundland dory. Smith also describes the early turtle industry.

290 **Archaeology of the Cayman Islands.**
   Roger C. Smith. *Archaeology*, vol. 36, no. 5 (Sept./Oct. 1983),
   p. 16-24.

This article outlines an archaeological survey conducted by the Institute of Nautical Archaeology from College Station, Texas. The first season of work began in May 1979 on Little Cayman where 17 individual sites were found. One site, dubbed the Turtle Wreck, is described in detail. The 1980 season began on Cayman Brac and moved to Grand Cayman. In total, 70 archaeological sites were recorded during the two seasons of study.

History

Caribbean/West Indies

291 The modern Caribbean.
Edited by Franklin W. Knight, Colin A. Palmer. Chapel Hill, North
Carolina: University of North Carolina Press, 1989. 382p. map.
bibliog.

This work, comprising thirteen essays by Caribbean studies specialists, provides a
background to the history and culture of the region. The essays deal with labour,
politics, the economy, literature, international relations, race and Caribbean migration.

292 A short history of the West Indies.
John Horace Parry, Philip Manderson Sherlock, Anthony P. Maingot.
New York: St. Martin's Press, 1987. 4th ed. 333p. bibliog.

First published in 1956, this work is a valuable introduction to West Indian history.
The authors begin with the arrival of Columbus and trace West Indian history through
to independence in most of the British Caribbean. They treat the study of the history
of the West Indies in its own right, rather than as an extension of the history of
Europe, Africa, Asia or the United States.

**293 Main currents in Caribbean thought: the historical evolution of
Caribbean society in its ideological aspects, 1492-1900.**
Gordon K. Lewis. Baltimore, Maryland: Johns Hopkins University
Press, 1983. 375p.

Lewis explores the sixteenth and seventeenth century beginnings of Caribbean
thought, pro- and anti-slavery ideologies, the growth of nationalist and anti-colonialist
sentiment in the nineteenth century and the development of secret religious cults. He
is able to show how European, African and Asian ideas have become Creolized and
Americanized, thereby creating a new ideology. Although there is no bibliography,
Lewis does provide a large section of notes.

294   **From Columbus to Castro: the history of the Caribbean, 1492-1966.**
Eric Eustace Williams.   New York: Harper & Row, 1970. 576p. 3 maps. bibliog.

Williams, who was Prime Minister of Trinidad and Tobago from 1956 to 1981, has written the first complete history of the Caribbean as a whole. His purpose was to collate all existing knowledge of the area in relation to the rest of the world and to provide, through a greater awareness of its heritage, a foundation for the economic integration of the region.

295   **The growth of the modern West Indies.**
Gordon K. Lewis.   New York: Monthly Review Press; London: MacGibbon and Kee, 1968. 506p. map. bibliog.

Lewis provides a descriptive and interpretive analysis of the English-speaking Caribbean from 1918 to 1966. This work, organized along territorial and thematic lines, analyses in detail the various elements that make up the whole of West Indian society. Lewis makes brief mention of the Cayman Islands with reference to the islands' constitutional status, economy, isolation, social life and turtle industry.

296   **History of the British West Indies.**
Alan Cuthbert Burns.   London: Allen & Unwin; New York: Barnes & Noble, 1965. 2nd ed. 849p. 30 maps. bibliog.

Burns' book is designed to give the general reader an outline history of the West Indies, from its discovery to 1964, with particular emphasis on the British West Indies. The work is based on source material and is well-documented. There are some references to the Cayman Islands and the hurricanes which passed through the West Indies.

General

297   **The '32 storm: eye-witness accounts and official reports of the worst natural disaster in the history of the Cayman Islands.**
Edited by Heather R. McLaughlin.   George Town: Cayman Islands National Archive, 1994. 187p. 4 maps.

The hurricane McLaughlin describes struck the Caymans on 7 November 1932 and lasted until 9 November. The author has used oral histories, written histories and contemporary photographs to produce a coherent and powerful narrative. In Part One, she describes the story of the storm. In Part Two, McLaughlin provides one section of letters, telegrams and reports, and a second section of songs and poems about the event.

298 **The wreck of the ten sails.**
Edited by Margaret E. Leshikar-Denton. George Town: Cayman
Islands National Archive and the Cayman Free Press, 1994. 78p.
2 maps. (Our Islands' Past, vol. II).

The wreck of ten ships, which formed part of a 58 merchant ship convoy, occurred on
8 February 1794. Numerous legends have sprung up around this incident and
Leshikar-Denton attempts to set the record straight. There is an excellent introduction
by the editor together with Philip Pedley of the National Archive. Leshikar-Denton
then provides fifteen historical documents about the convoy, the wreck and its
aftermath, including the transcript of the Court Martial of John Lawford, Captain of
the convoy's escort ship, H. M. S. Convert. All the documents are transcribed and
several are reproduced in facsimile. See also the editor's doctoral thesis *The 1794
'Wreck of the Ten Sail', Cayman Islands, British West Indies: A historical study and
archaeological survey* (1993. 577p. Texas A. and M.U.). [DAI 1994 54 (12): 4494-A.
DA 9411 296].

299 **Under tin roofs: Cayman in the 1920s.**
Aarona Booker Kohlman. Grand Cayman: Cayman Islands National
Museum, 1993. 120p. 2 maps.

Kohlman was born in Ohio in 1913. She lived in the Caymans from 1925 to 1928
while her father was a missionary there. These are her memoirs of those years, which
she calls 'an enchanted time'. Kohlman writes of boat launchings, bush medicine,
education, rope making and turtling. The accompanying photographs were taken by
her father. A glossary is also included.

300 **The lawless Caymanas: a story of slavery and freedom.**
Brian L. Kieran. Grand Cayman: The Author, 1992. 189p. bibliog.

This work is primarily a history of the West India Regiment's involvement in the
Cayman Islands. A detachment of the Second West India Regiment arrived in the
Cayman Islands in 1834 to keep the peace in case the masters rose in revolt at the time
of the British Proclamation of the Freedom of the Slaves (2 May 1835). The
Regiment's services were not needed for long. The detachment left on 3 June 1835.
Much of Kieran's work is based on primary sources, many of which are reproduced
and transcribed in this book. There are also excellent illustrations.

301 **Turtle isles: from turtles shells to offshore banks, the Cayman
Islands makes its mark.**
Sybil I. McLaughlin. *Parliamentarian*, vol. 73 (April 1992),
p. 116-17.

McLaughlin provides a brief history of the Cayman Islands, touching on navigators,
privateers and the islands' connections with Jamaica.

302 **Cayman yesterdays: an album of childhood memories.**
Heather R. McLaughlin. George Town: Cayman Islands National
Archive, 1991. 73p.

This is a collection of stories and reminiscences by 44 Caymanian narrators born
between 1888 and 1927. The information has been taken from the Cayman Islands

Memory Bank which has recorded over 300 tapes of more than 150 people. These fascinating narratives, illustrated with photographs from the Cayman Islands National Museum collection and many private collections, are arranged by topics such as fishing, picnics, playing, celebrating, etc.

303 **Bodden Town: first capital of the Cayman Islands.**
Harwell M. McCoy, Sr.   Bodden Town, Grand Cayman: Cayman Free Press, 1989. 1 vol. map.

This slim volume was prepared for the Bodden Town District Committee in honour of HRH Princess Alexandra's visit in 1989. McCoy provides a textual and photographic history of the town.

304 **Lest it be lost.**
Lee Alfonzo Ebanks.   Grand Cayman: The Author, 1985. 132p. map.

The author, who was born in 1905, writes of his life as a teacher, an inspector of police and a Justice of the Peace. This is a personal history, written for his family but expressive of life in the Caymans in the twentieth century.

305 **The sea of bitter beauty.**
Elsa M. Tibbetts.   St. Petersburg, Florida: The Author, 1984. 60p. 3 maps.

This is a non-academic, personal history by a woman born on Cayman Brac.

306 **A brief history of the Cayman Islands: a unique community 'founded upon the seas'.**
Alice Grant Bingner.   [S.I.] The Author, 1982. 22p.

In this very brief history, Bingner comments on the highlights of Caymanian history.

307 **A thesis on Cayman.**
Thomas C. Elder, Ann R. Elder.   Hamilton, Indiana: The Authors, 1975. 67p. bibliog.

This short history of the Cayman Islands also contains some information concerning Caymanian society. There are eight colour plates.

308 **A history of the Cayman Islands.**
Neville Williams.   Grand Cayman: Government of the Cayman Islands, 1970. 94p. 2 maps.

Williams, who was Deputy Keeper of Public Records in Great Britain at the time, wrote this book to mark the tercentenary of the Treaty of Madrid. He divides his history into four sections: From Columbus to the buccaneers (1503-1733); From permanent settlement to the end of slavery (1734-1834); A century of isolation (1834-1934); and The latest age (1934-1970). This is a good, concise history and a useful basis for further investigation.

309 **The 'Cayman Islands' of Samuel de Champlain de Bourage.**
Chapman Grant. *Isis*, vol. 38, pts. 1-2, nos. 111/112 (Nov. 1947),
p. 102-03.

Grant refutes Champlain's claim that he sailed to the 'Caymanes' Islands. He points out six errors in the Champlain text 'which made me believe that it was impossible for [Champlain] to be referring to the British Caymans.' (p. 103) A copy of Champlain's map of the 'Isles Caymanes' has been inserted between pages 102 and 103.

310 **Notes on the Cayman Islands.**
H. B. L. Hughes. *Jamaican Historical Review*, vol. 1, no. 2 (Dec. 1946), p. 154-58.

Hughes provides an excerpt from Records of the Royal Sociedad Patriotica of Havana, Volume V, printed in 1838. In this excerpt, Captain Don Juan Tirri describes a visit paid to the Isle of Pines in 1797. He was commissioned to prepare a report on conditions on the island by the Governor-General of Cuba. As part of his report, he writes of the strategic position Grand Cayman plays in the Caribbean and of the sea robbers who inhabit the Caymans. Captain Tirri recommends that the Spanish wipe out these pirate nests both on the Cayman Islands and on New Providence in the Bahamas. Hughes compares Captain Tirri's comments concerning lawlessness with correspondence between Governor Nugent of Jamaica and William Bodden of Bodden Town on Grand Cayman in 1802 and 1805.

311 **Notes on the history of the Cayman Islands.**
George Stephenson Shirt Hirst. Kingston, Jamaica: P. A. Benjamin Manufacturing Co., 1910; Grand Cayman: Caribbean Colour Ltd., 1967. 412p.

This work, upon which all future histories have been based, was originally published in three volumes. Some 1967 editions have been reprinted and bound as one volume of 412 pages and some have been reprinted and bound in three volumes. Volume One includes Part One, history from 1503 to 1734; Part Two, events and settlement from 1734 to 1800; and information and commentary on early families and settlements. In Part One, Hirst includes a great many extracts from British documents where there is any mention of the Cayman Islands. Part Two also includes transcriptions of wills, indentures and deeds. Volume Two includes Part Three, history from 1800 to 1850, and information on slavery, immigrants, ships and shipping, and religion. In this section, Hirst has provided transcriptions of manumission documents and deeds of transaction. There is also a section on administration and the courts which includes court documents and acts. Volume Three (Parts Four and Five) includes history from 1850 to 1909 and information on immigrants, shipping, turtling, storms and hurricanes, medical history, religion, ornithology and economic botany. Again, a number of documents are reproduced. An appendix lists Justices of the Peace (1856-1910), Clerks of the Courts (1855-1910), visits of Governors of Jamaica (1868-1909) and shopkeepers on the islands in 1910. Hirst has written a valuable history of the Cayman Islands, though the information is not always easily accessible. It is also a useful source of genealogical data.

312 **Cayman Brac: land of my birth.**
H. C. Dixon. Brooklyn, New York: Shining Light Survey, n.d. 55p.
Dixon writes of the early settlers on Cayman Brac and their quest to establish lives for themselves and future generations. There is also information on medical services, schools, industry and the seafaring life.

Cayman Islands and Jamaica

313 **The story of Jamaica from prehistory to the present.**
Clinton Vane de Brosse Black. London: Collins, 1965. rev. ed. 255p. 2 maps. bibliog.
Based on his *History of Jamaica*, published in 1958 (London: Collins, 256p.), Black has concentrated on telling the island's story from prehistory to independence in 1962 in as much detail as possible without interpreting that story for his readers. Although there is little information about the Cayman Islands, this is a good readable history of Jamaica which will provide background information for the study of the relationship between Jamaica and the Cayman Islands.

314 **A history of Jamaica from its discovery by Christopher Columbus to the year 1872.**
William James Gardner. London: Stock, 1873; New York: Appleton, 1907; London: Cass, 1971. 510p. map. (Cass Library of West Indian Studies, no. 17).
Gardner's work is one of the most detailed histories of Jamaica written in the post-emancipation period. Gardner, a missionary and pastor in Jamaica from 1849 to 1874, divides Jamaican history into five major periods. Under each there are chapters devoted to historical events, commerce and agriculture, religion and education, and manners and customs. Like Black's *The story of Jamaica* . . . (q.v.), this work is useful for background information.

Politics and Government

315 **Cayman Islands.**
Gary Brana-Shute, Rosemary Brana-Shute. In: *Political parties of the Americas, 1980s to 1990s: Canada, Latin America, and the West Indies.* Edited by Charles D. Ameringer. Westport, Connecticut: Greenwood Press, 1992, p. 167-68.

This short article explains the government structure in the Cayman Islands. There are no formal political parties. A short-lived political party system emerged in the early 1960s but disappeared within a few years. Individual candidates represent political clubs or 'teams'.

316 **The Cayman Islands: the evolutionary approach to political development.**
Sybil I. McLaughlin. *Parliamentarian*, vol. 73 (April 1992), p. 113-15.

McLaughlin, the first Speaker of the Cayman's Legislative Assembly, provides a brief history of the government of the islands and outlines constitutional changes and growth. She feels that the parliamentary system leads to national stability and sustained development. Like most Caymanians, she would like more control over internal affairs but does not wish to have independence from Great Britain.

317 **Conflict of interest: the case for a written code of ethical conduct in the Cayman Islands.**
W. McKeeva Bush. *Parliamentarian*, vol. 73 (April 1992), p. 119-20.

Bush, a Member of the Cayman's Legislative Assembly, argues for the adoption of, and the adherence to, a written standard of behaviour for all Caymanian politicians.

318 **Keeping in touch: representing the people in a small constituency.**
Roy Bodden. *Parliamentarian*, vol. 73 (April 1992), p. 122-23.
In discussing the role of a politician in relation to his constituents, Bodden, a Member of the Cayman's Legislative Assembly, also provides a look at election campaigning in the islands. In addition he outlines a representative's activities in the Legislative Assembly.

319 **A special son: the biography of Ormond Panton.**
David Martins. George Town: Pansons, Ltd., 1992. 215p.
A biography of Ormond Panton (1920-1992), the Caymanian lawyer and politician. Panton was first elected as a Vestryman in the 1940s and eventually became president of the National Democratic Party, which was formed in 1961 as part of a campaign for self-government. This political party, along with its conservative opposition, the Christian Democratic Party, disappeared within a few years.

320 **Team politics: making a trusted parliamentary system work.**
Benson O. Ebanks. *Parliamentarian*, vol. 73 (April 1992), p. 121.
Ebanks, a Member of the Cayman's Executive Council, outlines the election procedures and the parliamentary system as they are practiced in the Cayman Islands.

321 **Steele recycled.**
Judy Steele. Grand Cayman: Cayman Free Press, 1991. 152p.
Judy Steele's editorial cartoons began appearing in the Friday issue of the *Caymanian Compass* (q.v.) in 1987. The collection of cartoons reproduced in this volume, was created between 1987 and 1991 and reflects the politics of the islands.

322 **Government administration in a small microstate: developing the Cayman Islands.**
John E. Kersell. *Public Administration and Development*, vol. 7, no. 1 (Jan./March 1987), p. 95-107.
Kersell investigates administrative problems within the government of the Cayman Islands. He concludes that the dependence on outsiders needs to be reduced through human resource planning; that education and training for public service is inadequate; that control of administration is weak; and that political manipulation in personnel matters adversely affects performance.

323 **Chapelle's Compass capers.**
Bing Chapelle. George Town: Cayman Free Press, 1984? 24p.
A collection of 40 editorial cartoons published in the *Caymanian Compass* (q.v.) prior to 1984.

324 **Development of parliamentary government in the Cayman Islands specially prepared for the celebration of the 150th anniversary.**
Sybil I. McLaughlin. Grand Cayman: Cayman Free Press, 1981. 47p.
This anniversary publication contains information and commentary on the Chief Magistrates or Custos, the Legislative Assembly, the Clerks, royal representation and constitutional changes.

325 **The Governor of Cayman: an office in transition.**
John E. Kersell. *The Parliamentarian*, vol. 61 (1980), p. 91-94.
The purpose of this article is 'to suggest that . . . Cayman may recently have begun a transition, especially in the office of the Governor, that is now all but complete in Canada and other independent Commonwealth countries.' (p. 92). Kersell provides some constitutional background and describes the absolute authority of the Governor. He outlines recent practice whereby more power has devolved to the Executive Council. He concludes by describing the flexible and open decision-making style of the Governor, Mr. Thomas Russell, who held office between 1974 and 1982.

326 **Caymanian politics: structure and style in a changing island society.**
Ulf Hannerz. Stockholm: Universitetet Socialanthropologiska Institutionen, 1974. 198p. map. bibliog. (Stockholm Studies in Social Anthropology, 1).
Hannerz, an anthropologist, relates Cayman political events to social history and change. In Chapter One, he discusses the major historical characteristics of Cayman social and political life. Chapter Two outlines Caymanian society and politics from 1945. Chapter Three talks of current development and discord, while Chapter Four provides Hannerz' own views and summaries of what he has observed.

327 **You and your government: a publication of the Cayman Islands government.**
Cayman Government Information Service. Portsmouth, England: Eyre & Spottiswode, 1972. 81p.
This booklet describes the organization of government in the Cayman Islands. There are chapters detailing the Executive Council, the Legislative Assembly, the Public Service Commission, general administration, government departments and the Government Information Service. There is also a chapter outlining the islands' constitutional history.

328 **The Cayman Islands and its legislature.**
Sybil I. McLaughlin. *The Table*, vol. 33 (1964), p. 81-84.
This history of the government and administration of the Cayman Islands from the 18th century to the 1960s, was written by the author when she was Clerk of the Legislative Assembly and Executive Council. The article provides a good, if brief, introduction to the subject.

329 **The civil servant in the Cayman Islands.**
H. M. McCoy. *Social Scientist*, vol. 1 (Dec. 18, 1963), p. 6, 12.
In this short political history of the Cayman Islands, McCoy provides an overview of the civil service in the islands and puts forward an argument in favour of greater respect for the service.

Constitution and Legal System

Constitution

330 Cayman Islands: report of the Constitutional Commissioners, 1991.
Frederick Smith, Walter Wallace. London: HMSO, 1991. 21p. (Cm. 1547).

After an initial section containing background information for the Cayman Islands, the Commissioners discuss the 1972 constitution, which was based on the 1971 constitutional report prepared by the Earl of Oxford and Asquith (q.v.), and the amendments of 1984 and 1987. They also outline the political, social and economic developments which have occurred since 1972. Their major recommendations, which constitute the bulk of this report, touch on a Bill of Rights, the post of Governor, the Executive Council, the post of Chief Minister, the Legislative Assembly, the Finance Committee, the Speaker and the post of Leader of the Opposition. There are also several minor recommendations concerning referenda, the Public Service Commission, the Judiciary and the posts of Attorney-General and Auditor-General.

331 Cayman Islands: proposals for constitutional advance; report.
Great Britain. Constitutional Commissioner for the Cayman Islands.
London: HMSO, 1971. 30p.

This report was undertaken by the Earl of Oxford and Asquith. The five chapters in the main body of the work outline the islands' history and background, the present constitution and its predecessors, reflections on the consultations which were undertaken, the Earl's principal recommendations and his minor recommendations. Appendix I is a report of the Cayman's Legislative Assembly's Select Constitution Committee, while Appendix II is a minority report of the same committee.

Legal system

332   Criminal procedure in the Cayman Islands.
Piers Hill.   Oxford, England: Law Reports International, 1992. 230p.
This reference book was originally written for students of the Cayman Islands Law School. Hill examines the rules and procedures of the criminal courts, with examples from local legislation and local case law. The procedures are similar to English procedures with local idiosyncrasies, which Hill highlights in the appropriate and relevant passages. Hill does not evaluate Cayman law, but does feel that this and future research into the law will reveal, and ultimately correct, the inequities which do exist.

333   The legal system of the Cayman Islands.
Elizabeth W. Davies.   Oxford, England: Law Reports International, 1989. 214p.
Davies examines the developments which have occurred in the law and the government of the Cayman Islands over the last 300 years and shows how a comprehensive legal system has evolved to meet the needs of a modern society. The book contains information on the system of government and the legal system; legislation in the Caymans, both local and from the United Kingdom; the Courts of Justice; and the legal profession. Appendices outline statutes, court statistics from 1955 to 1985, population growth from 1774 to 1985, legislative output from 1865 to 1985 and law reporting in the country. Davies' book is based on her Master of Laws thesis submitted to University College, Cardiff, the University of Wales, in 1986.

334   Cayman Islands consolidated index of statutes and subsidiary legislation to . . .
Faculty of Law Library. University of the West Indies. Barbados.
Cave Hill, Barbados: Faculty of Law Library, 1986-. annual.
This is one of a series in the West Indian Legislation Indexing Project (WILIP), compiled in co-operation with the British Development Division.

335   Cayman Islands law reports.
Edited by Alan Milner, Marie-Louise McDonnell.   Oxford, England: Law Reports International, 1986-. annual.
These reports contain the cases heard before the Grand Court (the superior court of record) and the Court of Appeal. Each volume contains a list of judiciary and law officers, the cases reported, the cases cited, the legislation construed and a subject-matter index.

336   Paget-Brown's commercial law of the Cayman Islands.
Ian Paget-Brown.   Grand Cayman: Cayman Island Publishers, 1985. 2nd ed. 251p. bibliog.
Paget-Brown, who practices law in the Cayman Islands and the United States, presents his commentary on commercial law through a question and answer format. There are twelve chapters outlining twelve different laws pertaining to commerce and business

in the Cayman Islands. He also provides a list of the laws and the cases to which he refers throughout the book. This is a novel and useful way in which to present complex legal information to laypeople.

337   A guide to the laws of the Cayman Islands: with critical commentary.

Roderick N. Donaldson.   Hialeah, Florida: Peninsular Promotions, Inc., 1981. 136p.

Donaldson's book contains three major sections: the constitution of 1972; an index of current laws to December 1980; and an index of applied laws to December 1980. Each section includes its own separate commentary.

338   A concise guide to the Cayman Islands Companies Law.

Paul Harris.   Grand Cayman: International Directions, 1980. 2nd ed.

The first edition of this book was published in 1975, but there do not appear to have been any further editions after 1980. The book contains twenty chapters covering all aspects of company law. It is meant to be a quick and easy guide and reference to the law for practitioners; a complete and concise guide for foreign investors; and an educational source for law students.

Population

339 Edward Corbet's report and census of 1802 on the Cayman Islands.

George Town: Cayman Islands National Archive and the Cayman Free Press, 1992. 46p. (Our Islands' Past, vol. I).

Corbet was sent in 1802 by Governor Nugent of Jamaica as a special envoy to examine, among other things, the 'population, extent and Commerce' of the Cayman Islands. Part One of this publication contains a full transcript of his report, the census of 1802 and Nugent's comments. Corbet's report (p. 3-8) is in the form of a letter. The census (p. 10-23) is given both in facsimile form and transcription. Part Two consists of six relevant letters from the Nugent Papers.

340 Cayman Islands 1989 census.

Cayman Islands. Government Statistics Office. Grand Cayman: Government Statistics Office, 1990. 2 vols.

The 1989 census was the tenth census conducted in the Cayman Islands and was administered on 15 October 1989. Volume One provides a comprehensive summary of the census and includes commentary and tables of general interest. Volume Two is the administrative report. This volume outlines the planning and execution of the census, the post-enumerative fieldwork, coding and compiling, quality control and considerations for the next census. A proposed Volume Three was to have been the technical supplement to Volume One and would have provided additional detailed tables. It does not appear to have been published.

341 Population census 1979.

Grand Cayman: Cayman Islands, 1979. 354p. 10 maps.

This document is divided into thirteen sections corresponding to the Cayman Islands' thirteen census districts. There are 315 tables of statistics in total.

342 1970 population census of the Commonwealth Caribbean: 7 April and 25 October.

Mona, Jamaica: Census Research Programme, University of the West Indies, 1973. 10 vols.

These volumes contain statistics for age, economic activity, internal migration, education, race and religion, fertility, union status and marriage and households. Volume 4, part 13 contains eight tables of figures for the Cayman Islands.

Folklore

343 **The way we were or duppies: a Caribbean phenomenon.**
Richard F. Goldberg. *Journal of Psychological Anthropology*, vol. 2,
no. 2 (Spring 1979), p. 197-212.

A duppy is the shadow which lingers after death. In this paper, Goldberg examines the
relationship between the duppy and the living. He tries to show that the duppy is
related to kinship patterns in Grand Cayman and that the attitudes towards duppies
reflect attitudes towards close family members. Goldberg has included background
information and a review of the literature of duppies and jumbies (ghosts or evil
spirits) in the West Indies, along with several Cayman duppy stories.

344 **Duppies is.**
Robert Sevier Fuller. Georgetown: Cayman Authors, 1967. 73p.

On the cover, the author explains that this booklet is, 'an exposé of the caprices of
ghosts of Grand Cayman and a dictionary of words and phrases of the Islanders'.
Fuller interviewed a number of Caymanians in order to gather accounts of duppy
encounters. The interviews have been heavily edited, not in order to change their
content but rather to eliminate all traces of dialect. The appendix to the book is a list
of Caymanian words and expressions.

Religion

345 **The rise of the Seventh-Day Adventist Church in the Bahamas and the Cayman Islands.**
Jeffrey K. Thompson.   Nassau, Bahamas: The Author, 1992. 182p. map.

The Seventh-Day Adventist Church was established in the Cayman Islands in 1894. The information on the Cayman Islands (p. 97-170) is divided into decades and focuses primarily on the 1920s to 1990s. The text is accompanied by black-and-white photographs of churches and church leaders.

346 **A brief history of the Church of God in the Bay Islands of Honduras and the Cayman Islands.**
Will T. Bodden.   Grand Cayman: The Author, 1990. 38p.

Bodden provides information on the establishment of the denomination and early workers in the church.

347 **Cayman emerges: a human history of long ago Cayman.**
S. O. 'Bertie' Ebanks.   George Town, Grand Cayman: Northwester Co., Ltd., 1983. 78p.

Although Ebanks does provide some stories about wrecks, turtling and obeah (a form of voodoo practiced in some of the islands of the British West Indies), his real focus is on the history of religion in the islands.

348 **Cayman Islands Baptist centennial 1886-1986.**
Grand Cayman: s.n., n.d. 1 vol.

The Baptist Church was established in the Cayman Islands in 1886 by the Reverend W. H. Rutty, the first resident missionary. This slim volume gives a great deal of information about the history of the Baptist Church in the Cayman Islands and the early church workers.

349   **Presbyterian Church in Grand Cayman, 1846-1946.**
      Grand Cayman: s.n., n.d. 18p.

The first Presbyterian minister on the island was James Elmslie (1796-1864) who arrived in 1846. This small booklet was produced as a memento of the centenary of the work of the Presbyterian Church in Grand Cayman. It contains a good deal of information about the first one hundred years of the Presbyterian Church in the islands. There is also information about churches and religion on the island prior to 1846. The booklet concludes with lists of the Presbyterian ministers from 1846 in George Town, from 1857 in Boddentown and from 1913 in West Bay.

Social Conditions

350 **Cultural differences in preference for shapes.**
Krystyna Sierzant. *Perceptual and Motor Skills*, vol. 55, no. 3, pt. 1 (Dec. 1982), p. 991-94.
Sierzant surmised that since there is less sexual restraint in Jamaica, the sex difference for shape preference (males for female shapes, females for male shapes) would be greater for native Jamaicans than native Caymanians. The results supported Sierzant's supposition. Caymanian females preferred female shapes, while Jamaican females preferred male shapes. Caymanian males indicated no preference. Rastafarian Jamaican males preferred male shapes; non-Rastafarian Jamaican males preferred female shapes.

351 **The concept of household in East End, Grand Cayman.**
Richard Steven Goldberg. *Ethnos*, vol. 41, no. 1-4 (1976), p. 116-32.
Goldberg presents data from the 78 households he surveyed in East End, one of six districts on Grand Cayman. The purpose of his study was to introduce into the literature data on a society concerning its family and household structure. Such information has not previously been discussed with regard to Grand Cayman.

352 **The Cayman Islands.**
Middleton Wilson. In: *Human resources in the Commonwealth Caribbean*. Edited by Jack Harewood. St. Augustine, Trinidad: University of the West Indies, Institute of Social and Economic Research, 1970, p. 3b-1-3b-3.
This chapter forms part of the Report of the Human Resources Seminar held at the Mona Campus of the University of the West Indies in August 1970. Wilson points out that modern development in the Cayman Islands has been hampered by a shortage of manpower. After World War II many Caymanian males over the age of 17 left the islands to work on U. S. ships flying flags of convenience and on National Bulk Carriers. The manpower shortage led to the importation of labour, higher wages and inflation. It also resulted in a higher number of females entering the work force.

353 **Caymanian folk racial categories.**
Ira R. Buchler. *Man*, vol. 62 (Dec. 1962), p. 185-86.
This short article discusses and illustrates a series of racial categories used by African and mixed group Caymanians. The analysis of such folk racial categories permits a more accurate characterization of the islands' social reality.

354 **Intelligence tests of white and colored school children in Grand Cayman.**
Margaret Wooster Curti. *Journal of Psychology*, vol. 49, no. 1 (Jan. 1960), p. 13-27.
Tests were conducted in 1940 to determine whether successes and failures in intelligence tests were the result of economic and educational inferiority. In 3 out of 5 performance tests there were no significant differences between white and 'coloured' children. Similarly, there were no differences in number relationship tests and no differences in reasoning tests. Curti concludes that there is no support for the theory that inferiority in intelligence tests has a racial basis.

Health and Medicine

355   **The deaf of Grand Cayman, British West Indies.**
William Washabaugh.   *Sign Language Studies*, no. 31 (Summer
1981), p. 117-34.
In this study of the deaf community of Grand Cayman, Washabaugh provides
background information concerning the community's development and describes
Caymanian sign language and its relation to the sign language used on Providence
Island, off the Caribbean coast of Nicaragua.

356   **Anemia in the Cayman Islands: its prevalence and control.**
W. K. Simmons, D. P. Sinha.   Kingston, Jamaica: Caribbean Food
and Nutrition Institute, 1980. 33p. map. bibliog.
This study was undertaken to assess the prevalence of anaemia in the Cayman Islands
and to develop a programme to control the disease. The researchers found that during
pregnancy, anaemia was less prevalent in these islands compared to other Caribbean
islands. Also, they established that anaemia was dietary in origin and most prevalent
among infants. The report concludes with ten recommendations for the control of
anaemia.

357   **Preliminary report on detection and elimination programme on
cervical cancer in the Cayman Islands.**
J. E. Ayre, J. T. Burrowes.   *West Indian Medical Journal*, vol. 17,
no. 1 (March 1968), p. 21-25.
This report analyses the results of a cervical cancer study undertaken in 1966 in which
smears were taken from 931 women. Of that number, seventeen were found to have
cervical cancer. The authors describe the methodology and documentation of the
study, as well as the results of surgical follow-up.

358 **Caymanian folk medicine: a problem in applied anthropology.**
Ira R. Buchler. *Human Organization*, vol. 23, no. 1 (Spring 1964),
p. 48-49.

Buchler illustrates the importance to Caymanians of the form (e.g. liquid or solid) of folk medicine they receive. Studies have shown that Caymanians have been culturally conditioned to expect the administration of liquids, not solids, when illness strikes. Buchler's study arose from clashes between purveyors of folk medicine and western physicians.

359 **Inbreeding in an isolated island community.**
Edwin Beal Doran, Jr. *Journal of Heredity*, vol. 43, no. 6 (Nov./Dec.
1952), p. 263-66.

Doran gives a general description of the population of all the islands with an emphasis on two physical impairments: a particular type of tooth decay and deaf-mutism. He concludes that they are due to a high rate of consanguinity, particularly among the white population.

Economy

360 Economic development plan, 1986-1990.
Cayman Islands. Grand Cayman: Cayman Islands, 1986. 221p.
In 1985 the Legislative Assembly called for a five year economic development plan. The result is the most detailed and comprehensive survey which the government had ever undertaken with regard to the islands' future. The document contains background information and major plans for infrastructure, economic and social development. There are also plans for the development of other government services and detailed guidance concerning the implementation of all the recommended activities.

361 Caribbean economic handbook.
Edited by Peter D. Fraser, Paul Hackett. London: Euromonitor, 1985. 241p. 10 maps.
The section on the Cayman Islands (p. 168-72) provides information on the domestic economy, agriculture, industry, finance, tourism and trade. There are also statistical tables with data on financial institutions from 1979 to 1982; tourist arrivals in 1980 and 1981; imports by country of origin for 1975 and 1980; and vital statistics for 1984.

362 Marginal entrepreneurship and economic change in the Cayman Islands.
Ulf Hannerz. *Ethnos*, vol. 38, no. 1-4 (1973), p. 101-12.
Hannerz offers three case studies of individuals engaged in new small business enterprises which have in some way been influenced by the effects that tourism has had on the social and economic structure of the islands. Only one of the businesses profiled is actually tourist-related.

363 The Cayman Islands: an economic survey.
Barclays Bank. London: Barclays Bank D. C. O., 1971. 23p. map.
This survey provides information on history, climate, population, the constitution, the judicial and legal system, land and agriculture, occupations, trade and production,

tourism, currency and banking, finance and taxation, companies and trusts, communications, utilities, social services, the cost of living and immigration.

364 **Cayman Islands.**
    Donald H. Leavitt. *Foreign Trade*, vol. 132, no. 6 (Sept. 13, 1969),
    p. 14-16.
Leavitt, Assistant Trade Commissioner with the Canadian High Commission in Kingston, Jamaica, provides information for companies interested in establishing a foothold in the Cayman Islands. The information given should be used for historical reasons only, as it is clearly not current. Most data are from 1967.

365 **The Cayman Islands: economic survey and projections.**
    Great Britain. British Development Division in the Caribbean. Ministry
    of Overseas Development.   Bridgetown, Barbados: The Division,
    1969. 102p.
This survey was prepared to provide a basis for a five-year economic plan, 1970-75 and to provide a framework for discussions on future aid and loan requirements. The text (p. 1-49) contains sections on the economy, agriculture, fishing, manufacturing, construction, finance, transport, tourism and government. The statistical appendix (p. 51-102) contains 37 tables with figures from the 1960s. All dollar figures quoted are in Jamaican dollars, the legal currency at the time.

366 **An economic survey of the colonial territories 1951.**
    Great Britain. Colonial Office.   London: HMSO, 1953. vol. 4,
    p. 154-63.
Information for the Cayman Islands is contained in volume 4 (West Indian and American territories). There is textual and statistical information on geography, population, social services, political structure, economic legislation, production activities, finance and trade and development. There are also 19 tables of data which give figures for selected years from 1938 to 1951.

Finance and Banking

367 Cayman Islands.
Euromoney, supplement, The 1994 guide to offshore financial centres, (Nov. 1994), p. 40-48.

The Cayman Islands section of this guide contains information on the Cayman financial centre in general, the economic and regulatory infrastructure, banking and trust companies, trusts, mutual funds, insurance and captive insurance, companies and shipping. There is a chart which outlines government registration fees. The 1994 guide also includes Anguilla, the Bahamas, Bahrain, Barbados, Bermuda, the British Virgin Islands, Cyprus, Guernsey, Jersey, Madeira, the Netherlands Antilles and Puerto Rico. A similar guide was also produced in 1992 as a supplement to the May issue of *Euromoney*.

368 Cayman Islands.
Deloitte Touche Tohmatsu International.   George Town: Deloitte Touche Tohmatsu International, 1993. 57p. (International Tax and Business Guide).

This guide includes information on incentives and financing, foreign investment, foreign trade, business regulations, employment law and practice, accounting and auditing procedures and taxation. It is similar in style to booklets issued by Price Waterhouse (q.v.) and Ernst & Young (q.v.).

369 Doing business in the Cayman Islands.
Price Waterhouse World Firm.   Grand Cayman: Price Waterhouse World Firm, 1993. 68p.

This booklet was first published in 1971, with further editions published in 1978 and 1986. The current edition contains information on the business environment, foreign investment and trade opportunities, the regulatory environment, banking and finance, offshore companies, importing and exporting, labour relations and social security, audit requirements and practices, accounting principles and practices and the tax system. There is also a general profile of the country with information on geography and climate, history, the political structure, the legal system and population. All information is current to 1 August 1992.

370 **Pleasures of the Caribbean.**
Jonathan Burton. *Far East Economic Review*, vol. 155, no. 9 (March 5, 1992), p. 42-43.
Burton discusses and compares the offshore advantages of the Bahamas, Bermuda, the British Virgin Islands, the Cayman Islands, Nevis, Panama and the Turks and Caicos Islands.

371 **Where the money washes up.**
Steve Lohr. *New York Times Magazine* (March 29, 1992), p. 26-29, 32, 46, 52.
Lohr provides a detailed description of the banking industry in the Cayman Islands. He also discusses the role of the Cayman Islands offshore banking industry in the Bank of Credit and Commerce International (BCCI) scandal and collapse, and outlines outside attempts, especially from the United States, to gain access to banking records in the Cayman Islands.

372 **Doing business in the Cayman Islands.**
Ernst & Young. George Town, Grand Cayman: Ernst & Young, 1991. 40p.
This booklet provides information on the business environment, taxation, government controls and regulations, tourism, labour, accounting and reporting, as well as general information about living in the Cayman Islands.

373 **A financial centre with a low profile.**
Norman Peagam. *Euromoney*, supplement (May 1989), p. 55-60.
This overview discusses offshore banking, captive insurance and the promotion of ship registry. The article is followed by sponsorship statements under the general title, 'Cayman Islands: joining the world's finance centres' (p. 61-72). Contents of this section include: 'Stable Cayman reaps its rewards' (p. 63-66); 'Future growth that doesn't scare the world' (p. 67); 'Cayman retains its universal appeal' (p. 68-70); 'Treasure islands in tranquil waters' (p. 71); and a map (p. 72).

374 **Cayman National Bank: local pace-setter.**
David Jones. *The Banker*, vol. 134, no. 699 (May 1984), p. 50-51.
This short article about the Cayman National Bank was written ten years after its inception.

375 **US shadow over the Caymans.**
David Jones. *The Banker*, vol. 134, no. 699 (May 1984), p. 43-44, 46-48, 50-51.
A United States court order requiring the Miami branch of the Bank of Nova Scotia (Scotiabank) to produce bank records from its Cayman Island branch prompted Jones to write this article about the Cayman Islands' confidentiality laws. An accompanying chart lists information about the 41 principal banks in the Cayman Islands, giving each

bank's address, the type of licence it holds, the name of the senior executive, the number of staff and the names of the principal shareholders.

376   **Cayman: boom with a guilt complex . . .**
         The Banker, vol. 133 (March 1983), p. 17-18.
This article discusses the problem of illicit money being 'laundered' through Cayman banks. It outlines the current policing legislation and controls and discusses the concerns over giving foreign government agencies access to bank records. On page 18 there is an advertisement, separate from the article, for the Cayman National Bank and Trust Co., Ltd. It gives the Bank's balance sheet for 31 October 1982, with asset and liability figures for 1981 and 1982.

377   **The Cayman Islands: islands of mixed blessings.**
         John Edwards.   *CGA Magazine,* vol. 17, no. 1 (Jan. 1983), p. 7, 35.
Edwards describes the lack of taxation, the special rules applicable to exempt companies, exempt trusts, and banking and trust company legislation.

378   **Cayman Islands: an *Investors Chronicle* survey.**
         Adrian Day.   *Investors Chronicle*, vol. 60, supplement (June 4, 1982),
         p. 1-36.
This survey contains eight short articles: 'The right climate for a tax haven'; 'Companies – almost as many as people'; 'Why Cayman attracts international banks'; 'Captive insurance – an essay in diversification' by Roger Corbin; 'Trusts – marked by simplicity and flexibility'; 'Tourism – going for a quality market'; 'Property – pause in growth'; and 'Welcome to investors' by Vassel Johnson.

379   **The Caymans – offshore banking paradise.**
         Richard B. Miller.   *Bankers Magazine*, vol. 164, no. 1 (Jan./Feb.
         1981), p. 39-42.
Miller describes the offshore banking industry and its growth, which he attributes to the stability of the islands and government encouragement. The article contains two tables which illustrate the growth of the industry from 1973 to 1979.

380   **Why bankers love the Cayman Islands.**
         Richard B. Miller.   *Business and Society Review*, no. 38 (Summer
         1981), p. 19-21.
This article outlines the growth and development of the banking industry and highlights the advantages and disadvantages of conducting financial business in the Cayman Islands.

381 **Focus on the Cayman Islands.**
Michael L. Alberga, Darryl Myers.   Grand Cayman: The Authors,
1980. 59p. map.

This early booklet was produced for foreign businesses interested in locating to the Cayman Islands. The authors provide information on banking and trusts, corporations and companies, linked partnerships, real estate, the registration of ships, insurance, patents and trade marks, the registration of aircraft, and residence and citizenship. There is also a business directory.

382 **The tax haven that Jim Macdonald built.**
Martin Keeley.   *Canadian Business Magazine*, vol. 52, no. 10 (Oct.
1979), p. 67-68, 70, 73.

Jim Macdonald, a Calgary lawyer and politician, first visited the Cayman Islands in 1959. He moved there permanently in 1960 and drafted the first Companies Law. This article discusses the legal aspects of establishing a company in the Cayman Islands and provides information on banking. There is also a separate section (p. 69) entitled 'Tax avoidance in the sun: a guide to the Caymans'.

383 **U. S. banks and the North American Euro-currency market.**
Rodney H. Mills, Jr., Eugene D. Short.   *Journal of Commercial Bank
Lending*, vol. 61, no. 11 (July 1979), p. 27-38.

The authors examine the impact which institutional and economic factors have had on the North American Euro-currency market, with particular reference to the offshore financial centres in the Bahamas and the Cayman Islands. There are two tables of data for 1973-1978.

384 **Financially flexible Cayman Islands.**
Royan D. Ellis.   *Tax Executive*, vol. 27, no. 1 (Oct. 1974), p. 9-16.

Ellis outlines why the Cayman Islands have developed into an important base for international financial operations. There is information on tax-free status, currency control, ordinary company rules, exempt companies, banks and trust companies, and captive insurance companies.

385 **When is a tax haven?**
A. B. McKie.   *Canadian Banker & ICB Review*, vol. 81, no. 4
(July/Aug. 1974), p. 46-48.

This is a light-hearted look at the Cayman Islands and its status as a tax haven/tax shelter or, as McKie terms it, tax heaven.

386 **The Caymans' cash crop.**
John Kirkaldy.   *New Statesman*, vol. 85, no. 2200 (May 18, 1973),
p. 729-30.

Kirkaldy writes about the boom in the Cayman Islands' economy, particularly in the growth of tourism and the increase in banks and trust companies. He also discusses the problems that have arisen: traffic congestion and increases in crime and drug prosecutions. The cash crop referred to in his title is tax evasion.

387 **Cayman Islands:** *Financial Times* **survey.**
John Bradley. *Financial Times* (Sept. 17, 1971), p. 27-33.

This early survey provides information on the economy, banking, real estate market, tax system, offshore companies, the newly established turtle farm and tourism.

388 **Estimates of revenue and expenditure of the Cayman Islands.**
Grand Cayman: Cayman Islands, 1951/52-. annual.

This annual publication provides financial figures for all government departments.

Industry, Trade and Labour

General

389 **Sir Turtle moving forward steadily.**
Douglas W. Nelms. *Air Transport World*, vol. 29, no. 3 (March 1992), p. 57-58, 61.
Nelms outlines the development and operations of Cayman Airways. Sir Turtle is Cayman Airways' logo.

390 **Grand Cayman Island and the resort cycle concept.**
David B. Weaver *Journal of Travel Research*, vol. 29, no. 2 (Fall 1990), p. 9-15.
The various stages in the development of tourism, as first proposed by R. W. Butler in 1980, are applied to Grand Cayman. Weaver discusses the exploration stage (up to the 1950s), the involvement stage (1950s to 1970s) and the development stage (from the 1970s to the present). There is also a table listing tourist arrivals from 1964 to 1986.

391 **Annual trade report.**
Cayman Islands. Department of Finance and Development. Grand Cayman: Government Statistics and Information Services, Department of Finance and Development, 1980?-. annual.
This report provides tables of statistics for balance of trade, imports and exports, and trade summaries.

392 **Cayman Islands natural resources study: results of the investigations into commercial fishing potential.**
A. J. Rae, R. N. Stevens. London: Ministry of Overseas Development, 1976. 57p. 3 maps. bibliog. (Cayman Islands Natural Resources Study, part V).

Rae and Stevens conclude that accessible stocks of some marketable fish are present in the waters surrounding the Cayman Islands and could be caught in sufficient quantity for local demand.

393 **The fisheries of Cayman Islands, report.**
Ernest Freeman Thompson. Bridgetown, Barbados: Advocate Co., 1946. 33p. (Great Britain. Comptroller for Development and Welfare in the West Indies. Bulletin, no. 22).

Despite the title of this report, Thompson focuses on the export trade of four main items: thatch rope, green turtles, hawksbill turtles and shark hides, and offers recommendations on how to rehabilitate and expand the economy of the islands. Thompson suggests that imports should be replaced with locally produced articles; training in handicrafts should be offered; existing industries should be expanded; new industries, especially fishing for export, need to be developed; social amenities and social services need to be improved; and tourism possibilities should be considered. There are three tables of statistics: population on January 4, 1943; the season for various fish in the waters of the islands; and exports of thatch rope, green turtles, hawksbill turtles and shark hides for the period 1914 to 1939. Thompson also provides a great deal of information on taxation, revenue and trade.

394 **Forestry in the Cayman Islands, report.**
Christopher Swabey, C. Bernard Lewis. Bridgetown, Barbados: Advocate Co., 1946. 31p. (Great Britain. Comptroller for Development and Welfare in the West Indies. Bulletin no. 23).

Swabey, the Conservator for Forests in Jamaica, and Lewis, Curator of the Museum at the Institute of Jamaica, visited Grand Cayman in 1945 in order to gather information for their report. The introductory section of the report (p. 5-13) offers a general description of the Cayman Islands. In the section on forests and forestry (p. 14-23), the authors provide information on vegetation types, current forest legislation and forest utilization, with charts outlining imports and exports from 1935 to 1944. This is followed by their recommendations (p. 24-27). They recommend that a general forest policy be established in order to conserve and develop forests for industrial and commercial purposes. They also suggest that to properly implement this policy, the government must conduct surveys, establish forest reserves, construct roads, draw up appropriate legislation, hire and train staff, and provide adequate finances. There are three appendices (p. 28-31): a proposed Forest Law; proposed regulations to be made under the Forest Law; and a chart showing annual shipments of straw rope to Jamaica from 1941 to 1945.

Turtle industry

395 Last chance lost? Can and should farming save the green sea turtle? The story of Mariculture, Ltd. – Cayman Turtle Farm.
Peggy Fosdick, Sam Fosdick.   York, Pennsylvania: Irvin S. Naylor, 1994. 338p. 5 maps. bibliog.

Mariculture, Ltd. was established in 1968 by English investors to raise turtles as an industry. It was purchased by German investors in 1975 and by the Cayman government in 1983. The first products were introduced in 1972: meat, shell, oil, leather and calipee, a substance which is derived from the turtle's belly plate and is the primary constituent in clear turtle soup. The Fosdicks describe the turtle farm's first quarter of a century of operation in great detail, outlining its survival against ever-changing and powerful odds. They conclude that turtle farming is and can continue to be a successful venture. The 14 appendices include a chronology, recipes and a bibliography.

396 The Cayman Turtle Farm.
Tom A. Walker.   *Aquaculture Magazine*, vol. 18, no. 2 (March/April 1992), p. 47-55.

Walker highlights the Cayman Turtle Farm's successes and failures and describes the breeding process.

397 Green turtle farming: a growing debate.
George Reiger.   *Sea Frontiers*, vol. 21, no. 4 (July/Aug. 1975), p. 215-23.

Reiger begins with a history of the turtle industry from 1503 and provides information on the development of Mariculture, Ltd., the turtle farming enterprise. He examines the debate between the supporters of commercial turtle farms and conservationists who believe that the turtles should be added to the endangered species list.

398 Now they're farming turtles.
Nancy Sefton.   *Oceans*, vol. 7, no. 5 (Sept./Oct. 1974), p. 34-35.

Sefton describes the activities of Mariculture, Ltd. and also provides some background information on turtling and the turtle industry.

399 Capturing giant turtles in the Caribbean.
David D. Duncan.   *National Geographic Magazine*, vol. 84, no. 2 (Aug. 1943), p. 177-90.

Duncan describes Cayman Islanders turtling off the Mosquito Coast of Nicaragua and taking their catches to Key West, Florida for sale. There are 13 black-and-white photographs and one map.

Statistics

400 Cayman Islands historical compendium of statistics, 1774-1980.
Cayman Islands. Government Statistics Office.   George Town, Grand
Cayman: Government Statistics Office, 1992. 71p.

The series of statistics listed in this publication have been gathered, for the most part,
from the annual *Statistical Abstract* (q.v.). Not all tables have figures going back as far
as 1774.

401 Cayman Islands compendium of statistics.
Cayman Islands. Economics and Statistics Office.   George Town,
Grand Cayman: Economics and Statistics Office, 1991-. annual.

This annual publication contains statistics on a wide variety of topics: agriculture,
education and culture, elections, employment, finance, foreign trade, health and social
services, housing, land and property transfers, population, prices and national income,
protective services, tourism, transport and communication, and utilities. It was
previously published as *Statistical Abstract of the Government of the Cayman Islands*
(q.v.).

402 Statistical abstract of the government of the Cayman Islands.
Cayman Islands. Government Statistics Office.   Grand Cayman:
Government Statistics Office, 1975-90. annual.

This publication gathers together statistical information on the Cayman Islands in one
volume for easy reference. Contents include area, population, vital statistics,
agriculture, forestry, fisheries, mining and manufacturing, labour and employment,
construction and housing, transport and communication, tourism, trade, consumer
prices, finances, education and health, planning and national income. The title was
changed to *Statistical Abstract of the Cayman Islands* in 1980.

Postal System

403 **Cayman Islands: the John Byl collection.**
London: Christie's, 1992. 27p.
This sale catalogue contains both colour and black-and-white plates for the 144 lots of Cayman stamps which were auctioned. The stamps cover the period from 1829 to 1962.

404 **The postal history of the Cayman Islands.**
Thomas E. Giraldi, Peter P. McCann.   Weston, Massachusetts: Triad Publications, 1989. 172p. bibliog.
Giraldi and McCann concentrate on areas of Cayman postal history other than stamps. This book examines a number of other aspects of postal history which are often neglected. The two authors have investigated cancellations, postage meters (which were introduced in 1970), official markings, instructional markings and registrations. There are also chapters on airmail, postal censorship and postal stationery.

405 **Catalogue of the award winning collection of the Cayman Islands offered by order of R. J. Edmondson, Esq.**
Harmers of London.   London: Harmers, 1988. 31p.
This catalogue, well-illustrated with black-and-white plates, lists the 173 lots which were offered for sale. The collection includes stamps from 1891 to 1962.

406 **The postage stamps of the Cayman Islands.**
Fred J. Melville.   Beverly, Massachusetts; Portland, Oregon: Severn-Wylie-Jewett, 1920. 22p. bibliog. (Booklet no. 33).
This early history of postage stamps and the postal service in the Cayman Islands concentrates on the first few years beginning with the Post Office Law in 1900, the same year in which Caymanian stamps were introduced. (Prior to this, Jamaican stamps had been used.) Melville provides a detailed history, describes early stamps and includes some information on postmarks.

407 **The Cayman Islands: their stamps and post office.**
Douglas B. Armstrong in collaboration with C. B. Bostwick,
A. J. Watkin.   London: Published for the Council of the Junior
Philatelic Society by H. F. Johnson, 1910. 24p. map. bibliog. (Stamp
Lover Booklets, no. 3).

Armstrong and his collaborators provide a detailed history of postage stamps, postal
stationery and postmarks in the Cayman Islands.

Languages and
Dialects

**408   The off-shore island Creoles: Providencia, San Andres and the
Caymans.**
William Washabaugh. In: *Central American English.*   Edited by John
Holm.   Heidelberg, Germany: Groos, 1983, p. 157-79. maps. bibliog.

This chapter is divided into two sections. The first deals with Providencia and San
Andres, islands 150 miles off the Caribbean coast of Nicaragua. In the second section
(p. 174-179), Washabaugh discusses the dialect found in the East End. He chose this
area of Grand Cayman because it was remote and the dialect would have been less
affected by outside influences. He provides a sociolinguistic history of the Cayman
Islands and a transcription, in dialect, of a dialogue between an 80-year-old white
couple. There are also notes to assist in understanding the dialect and a short
annotated bibliography.

409   Notes on an archaic island dialect.
Edwin Beal Doran, Jr.   *American Speech*, vol. 29, no. 1 (Feb. 1954),
p. 82-85.

Doran describes the Cayman Island speech as an archaic form of English with Spanish
forms, fragments of Negro dialect and expressions common to the southern United
States, along with a number of nautical terms. He provides examples of a few
expressions to indicate the flavour of Caymanian speech.

410   Wotcha say: an introduction to colloquial Caymanian.
Aarona Booker Kohlman.   Grand Cayman: Cayman ARTventures,
n.d. 45p. map.

This work, based on Kohlman's Master's thesis, is an attempt to record variations of
spoken English in the Cayman Islands and to trace the origins of that spoken English.
The book contains historical background, an outline of pronunciation characteristics, a
lexicon, a list of place names and an appendix of male and female given names.

Literature

Anthologies

411 **Our voice.**
Edited by Mary Rodrigues, Roy Murray. Grand Cayman: Cayman
Free Press, 1992. 60p.
This is a collection of original poems and short stories written by students of John
Gray High School between 1988 and 1992.

412 **In our own write: a collection of poetry & short stories.**
The Creative Writers Association of the Cayman Islands. Grand
Cayman: The Association, n.d. 45p.
A collection of poems and short stories primarily about the Caymans and island life.

Individual writers

413 **Cayman stories and other stuff.**
Don L. Dise. Grand Cayman: The Author, 1995. 116p.
Part One of this book contains seven poems and six short stories. Part Two contains
three autobiographical sketches.

414 **Beyond the iron shore.**
Bonnie-Lee E. Webster. George Town, Grand Cayman: The Author,
1991. 194p. map.
This is a novel about early Cayman life. Webster has also included a vocabulary of
Caymanian words and phrases.

415 Love children: inspirational poetry and discourses.
Bonnie-Lee E. Webster.   George Town, Grand Cayman: The Author, 1991. 34p.

Webster offers two discourses, one on angels and another on beatitudes, and fifteen poems.

416 The winner's words: a collection of poems.
Diana Stewart Walker.   Spanish Town, Jamaica: Printed in Jamaica by Rowe's Printery Ltd., 1990. 37p.

A collection of 48 poems on a variety of topics including island life, the outside world and Cayman people.

417 The magic sailboat.
Beverley Baker.   Grand Cayman: EDO Ltd., 1986. 154p.

In this children's work, four children explore the Cayman Islands on a magic boat. They encounter stories about pirates, diving, slavery, turtles, hurricanes, duppies, the government, fishing and shelling.

418 Cayman bear book.
Sandra van der Bol. Illustrated by Debbie Rose Chase van der Bol.
Grand Cayman: Sea Gypsy Enterprises, 1985. 1 vol. map.

This book of verse for children is illustrated with watercolours and pen-and-ink drawings.

419 Cayman duppy.
William Hezlep.   Studio City, California: Players Press, Inc., 1984.
14p. map. (The Travelers).

In this one-act play, two children visiting the island meet a polite young man who weaves a tale of buried treasure. This play is set in a cemetery on Grand Cayman.

420 On the island of Cayman.
Jackie Bodden Webb.   Grand Cayman: The Author, 1981. 86p.

This third person, fictionalized autobiography tells of one year in the author's life when she was a young girl. Webb writes with an authentic flavour about the island's traditions, food, songs and people.

421 Time longer dan rope: a three act play.
Frank Swarres McField.   Grand Cayman: CAMAC Publishing Co., 1979. 58p.

This play of social commentary is set in George Town in 1963.

422 **The Cayman adventures of Arthur and Orlee.**
Nancy Sefton. Illustrated by Aileen Smith.   Grand Cayman: Cayman Free Press, 1978. 44p. map.

In this children's story, Arthur and Orlee learn about the Cayman Islands by interacting with a variety of animals.

423 **Something about us: a book of poems.**
Curtis L. E. Barnett.   George Town, Grand Cayman: Northwester Publishing Co., 1976. 58p.

A collection of poems written between 1968 and 1976.

424 **Bits of coral.**
Blanche Crang.   [S.I.]: The Author, 1969. [20p.].

A slim volume of poetry extolling the virtues and beauty of the Cayman Islands.

425 **The invulnerable rulers of Banner Reef.**
Teppo Turen.   Grand Cayman: Caribbean Colour, 1966. 81p.

While on vacation in the Cayman Islands, Turen broke his ankle and had to extend his stay in order to recuperate. He became so fascinated with the islands and the tales of turtle schooners, ship wrecks and hurricanes, that he stayed on as a resident. This book is based on legend and relates the adventures of the Caymans and Cayman Islanders in the late 1700s.

426 **Mr. Nobody: the sophisticated duppy of South Sound Road.**
Kerry Eric Hudson.   North Miami Beach, Florida: Cayman Islands Information Center, 1966. 37p. 2 maps.

Hudson was four years old when *Mr. Nobody* was written. The title page does actually indicate that the book was written 'by Kerry Eric Hudson and his Daddy'. Although classified as children's fiction, this delightful book is a view of the Cayman Islands through the eyes of a child and his imaginary friend, Mr. Nobody. It is a good introduction to the Caymans, even for adults.

427 **Inside the reef.**
David Eugene Conolly.   Grand Cayman: The Author, n.d. 68p.

This is a collection of poetry giving descriptions of islands the author clearly loves.

428 **Island thoughts: poems of the Cayman Islands.**
Joy Brandon.   Grand Cayman: Cayman Free Press, n.d. 20p.

This is a slim volume of 22 poems describing the joys and delights of the Cayman Islands.

Foreign literature set in the Cayman Islands

429   Far Tortuga.
Peter Matthiessen.   New York: Random House, 1975. 408p.

Set in the Cayman Islands, Matthiessen's novel is, among other things, a treatise on turtling, an account of the dying days of sailing ships and a history of the islands. He writes in an impressionistic and unusual style with minimal descriptive prose. The dialogue, which is the work's greatest strength, is written in dialect. In his article 'Waves of change: Peter Matthiessen's Caribbean' (*Environmental Review*, vol. 11, no. 3 (1987), p. 223–30), John R. Cooley concludes that Matthiessen's novel accurately depicted the life of Cayman Island green turtle fishermen confronting modernisation during the 1960s.

430   Shark Island.
Maurice Edelmen.   London: Hamish Hamilton, 1967. 299p.

This is the story of a British administrator of a decaying Caribbean island who is under pressure to authorize a US-based development scheme. The professional difficulties encountered are combined with his own personal problems. Edelmen, a British Labour Member of Parliament at the time, visited the Cayman Islands prior to writing this novel. His trip is said to have inspired the book.

The Arts

431 **My markings: the art of Gladwyn K. Bush, Caymanian visionary intuitive.**
Henry D. Muttoo, Karl 'Jerry' Craig. Edited by David Martins.
Grand Cayman: Cayman National Cultural Foundation, 1994. 156p.

Bush began painting at the age of 62. Critics call her an intuitive artist, one who started late in life and who paints with self-described divine inspiration. Through an 'iconographic use of imagery' (p. 11), Bush explores primarily Biblical themes with some secular motifs emerging from her past. The reproductions include both her paintings and her house which she has decorated inside and outside in an extraordinary fashion. The plates are accompanied by quotes from the artist.

432 **F. J. Harquail Theatre.**
Michele LaRue. *Theatre Crafts*, vol. 20, no. 10 (Dec. 1986), p. 26-29, 38-40.

The F. J. Harquail Theatre, the home of the Cayman National Theatre Company, was opened in 1986. The shell of the theatre was designed and built by local Caymanian firms, while the interior was designed and constructed by Theatre Projects Consultants in Great Britain. The interior was then shipped to Grand Cayman and re-assembled inside the shell. LaRue's article provides construction details and specifications and lists the firms involved in design and construction. Prior to this, the Cayman National Theatre Company, founded in 1978, performed in the cocktail lounge of the Royal Palms Hotel.

Sports

433 Cayman golf: does it herald a new revolution?

Malcolm Campbell. *Golf Monthly*, vol. 75, no. 5 (May 1985),
p. 42-45.

In the early 1980s, Jack Nicklaus was asked to design a golf course on Grand Cayman.
There were only 88 acres set aside for the course and clubhouse, a hotel and marina,
and condominiums and villas. Campbell describes the short course that Nicklaus
designed and the 'short course' golf ball he designed to be used on the course.

434 Cayman Islands and Olympism.

Olympic Review, no. 182 (Dec. 1982), p. 761-62.

This is a short description of the Cayman Islands' involvement in the Olympic
movement. The Cayman Islands Olympic Committee was founded in 1973 and the
country's first appearance at the Olympic games was in 1976.

Food and Drink

435 **Seafood landfood: Cayman Islands cookery.**
Lucy Mott, ed.   Grand Cayman: Sea Gypsy Enterprises, 1984. 61p.
A collection of 59 recipes for seafood, landfood and sweets.

436 **Grand recipes from the Cayman Islands.**
Betty Potter, Earl Cullen Potter, Jr.   Friendswood, Texas: Potter
Publications, 1985. 59p.
This cookery book contains 55 recipes for appetizers, soups, salads and side dishes,
main courses, desserts and drinks. It is interspersed with snippets of history, fact and
folklore.

Newspapers and Periodicals

Newspapers

437 **Caymanian compass.**
Grand Cayman: Cayman Free Press, Ltd., 1965-. daily.
The *Caymanian Compass* is the islands' only daily newspaper, published from Monday to Friday. It provides a good balance of local, regional and international news. The newspaper was formed when the *Cayman Compass* combined with the *Caymanian Weekly.*

438 **The new Caymanian.**
Grand Cayman: Cayman Media Corporation Ltd., 1990-. weekly.
The New Caymanian is published every Friday. It contains articles more concerned with opinions on issues rather than news items.

Periodicals

439 **Newstar: the national news magazine of the Cayman Islands.**
Grand Cayman: Cayman Publishing Co., 1987-. monthly.
This well-illustrated, glossy magazine includes national and international articles. Most of the articles provide longer commentaries rather than fast-breaking news. They deal with such topics as business and commerce, government and politics, history, and social issues.

440 **Cayman executive: the magazine that means business in the
Cayman Islands.**
Grand Cayman: Cayman Publishing Co., 1993-. quarterly.

This glossy publication, containing a large number of advertisements, presents
information on finances, tourism and commerce.

Directories

441 Caribbean business directory.
Grand Cayman: Caribbean Publishing Company, 1987-. annual.
This directory provides a general overview of the Caribbean, together with individual sections for each country listed. Entries are included for all Caribbean countries, plus Belize, Florida (primarily the Miami area), Guyana, French Guiana (Guyane) and Venezuela. Individual country profiles include a map, quick statistical facts, and information on the government, economy, geography, population, transport, business addresses, leisure and trends within the country. The statistics given are current to 1990. A classified listing of businesses is arranged alphabetically by industry/service and then alphabetically by country.

442 The Cayman Islands Chamber of Commerce directory.
Cayman Islands Chamber of Commerce.   George Town: Cayman Free Press, Ltd., 1985-88. annual.
The directory is divided into three sections: the Chamber of Commerce committees and their activities, general Chamber matters and a directory of members. It was absorbed by *Cayman Islands Yearbook and Business Directory* (q.v.).

443 Cayman Islands yearbook and business directory.
Grand Cayman: Cayman Free Press, 1985-. annual.
This publication provides a wealth of information about the Cayman Islands and, of all the directories listed, is the one which should be included in any Caymanian collection. There are sections on the year in review, government administration, finance and investment, business and commerce, and real estate and development. There is a substantial Chamber of Commerce directory, a reference section covering all aspects of life in the islands and a separate business directory.

444 **Dictionary of Latin American and Caribbean biography.**
Edited by Ernest Kay. Ely, England: Melrose Press, 1971. 2nd ed. 458p.

This 'who's who' provides one alphabetic sequence of individuals by surname. There is no geographic access although the foreword indicates that individuals from the Cayman Islands are included. The first edition was published in 1969 under the title *Dictionary of Caribbean Biography*.

445 **Personalities Caribbean: the international guide to who's who in the West Indies, Bahamas, Bermuda.**
Kingston, Jamaica: Personalities, 1965-. irregular.

The section on the Cayman Islands lists people from a variety of fields including government, finance and industry.

Bibliographies

446 Bibliography of the Cayman Islands.
J. E. Davies. In: *The Cayman Islands: natural history and biogeography.* Edited by M. A. Brunt, J. E. Davies. Dordrecht, Netherlands: Kluwer Academic Publishers, 1994, p. 543-56. (Monographiae Biologicae, vol. 71).
This is a list of 519 publications, reports and theses on a variety of subjects. The entries are not annotated.

447 Commonwealth Caribbean government publications: bibliographies and acquisition aids.
Kirsti Nilse. *Government Publications Review*, vol. 7A, no. 6 (1980), p. 489-503.
Describes the acquisition aids and bibliographies for use by librarians in identifying the government publications of the Caribbean including the Cayman Islands.

Index

The index is a single alphabetical sequence of authors (personal and corporate), titles of publications and subjects. Index entries refer both to the main items and to other works mentioned in the notes to each item. Title entries are in italics. Numeration refers to the items as numbered.

Y

Map of Cayman Islands

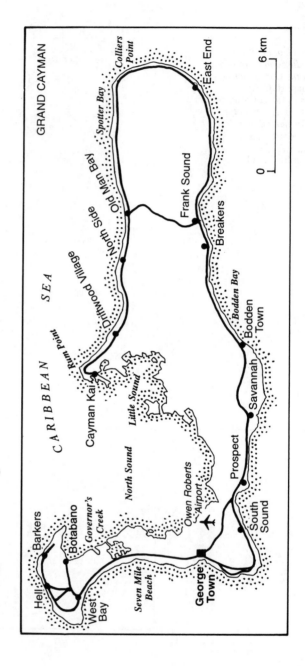

GRAND CAYMAN

CARIBBEAN   SEA

Hell
Barkers
West Bay
Botabano
Governor's Creek
Seven Mile Beach
North Sound
Rum Point
Cayman Kai
Little Sound
Driftwood Village
North Side
Old Man Bay
Spotter Bay
Colliers Point
Owen Roberts Airport
George Town
Prospect
South Sound
Savannah
Bodden Town
Bodden Bay
Breakers
Frank Sound
East End

0   6 km

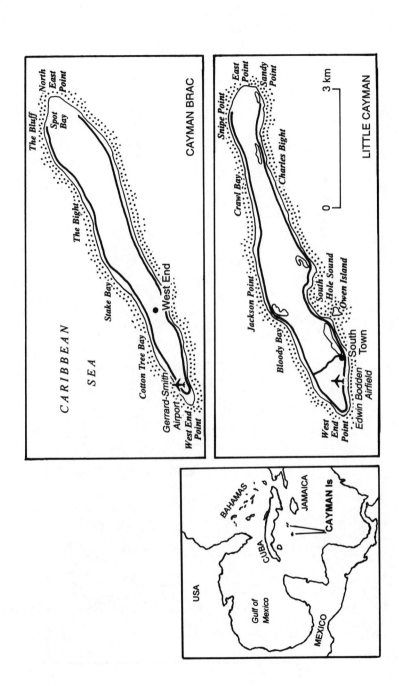

CARIBBEAN

SEA

The Bluff

North
East
Point

Spot
Bay

The Bight

Stake Bay

Cotton Tree Bay

Gerrard-Smith
Airport

West End

West End
Point

CAYMAN BRAC

Snipe Point

East
Point

Sandy
Point

Crawl Bay

Charles Bight

Jackson Point

Bloody Bay

South
Hole Sound

Owen Island

South
Town

Edwin Bodden
Airfield

West
End
Point

0   3 km

LITTLE CAYMAN

USA

Gulf of
Mexico

MEXICO

BAHAMAS

CUBA

JAMAICA

CAYMAN Is

ALSO FROM CLIO PRESS

INTERNATIONAL ORGANIZATIONS SERIES

Each volume in the International Organizations Series is either devoted to one specific organization, or to a number of different organizations operating in a particular region, or engaged in a specific field of activity. The scope of the series is wide-ranging and includes intergovernmental organizations, international non-governmental organizations, and national bodies dealing with international issues. The series is aimed mainly at the English-speaker and each volume provides a selective, annotated, critical bibliography of the organization, or organizations, concerned. The bibliographies cover books, articles, pamphlets, directories, databases and theses and, wherever possible, attention is focused on material about the organizations rather than on the organizations' own publications. Notwithstanding this, the most important official publications, and guides to those publications, will be included. The views expressed in individual volumes, however, are not necessarily those of the publishers.

VOLUMES IN THE SERIES

TITLE IN PREPARATION